MW01484518

Supervisor, Manager, Leader: The Basics of Being a Boss

A Common-Sense Approach to the Critical Skills That Most Organizations Fail to Teach Their People

by Mike Kraus

Copyright 2016 Mike Kraus

All rights reserved.

Cover Design by Sara Kraus

ISBN: 1537029215

ISBN: 9781537029214

Library of Congress Control Number: 2017901224

The contents of this book are based upon the author's personal experiences and beliefs. No guarantee is stated or implied as to the effectiveness of the concepts or techniques contained herein as applied by the reader.

This updated edition continues to be dedicated to my father and mother . . .

Ronald E. Kraus

1937–2016

Nancy J. Kraus

1940–2016

I would like to acknowledge and thank those individuals who, over the years, whether they realized it or not, served as my positive examples and mentors. Your efforts significantly contributed to my professional development as a supervisor, manager, and a leader.

I would also like to thank the following individuals for their personal support, honesty, thought-provoking discussion, and inspiration in the development of this project. Their passion for effective leadership is duly noted and appreciated:

Andrea Avila, Cara Elam, Tim Hankins, Tina Casola, John Short, and Jessica Smart.

Introduction

In April 2012, I retired after thirty-three years in the fire service. Twenty of those years were spent in positions where I was responsible for other employees. Was I the perfect supervisor, manager, or leader? Certainly not. I did, of course, continually try to improve myself in these areas. Unfortunately, what I did learn was pretty much accomplished on my own. My employer rarely, if ever, gave me any more than the very basics of training in these areas. That's probably why I teach up-and-coming fire officers with so much passion today. I don't want them to have to learn like I did. I want to teach them the skills they need to be successful. I want to teach them what I'm sure their own organizations won't bother to teach them.

I've always said that there should be a reference book and a corresponding course available to all of us as we entered different phases of our careers (as well as our lives, for that matter). It just seems to me that we have to learn lessons over and over, and we must do so unnecessarily—when the lessons have already been learned by those who have walked the same paths before us.

In order to avoid being a hypocrite, and to put my effort where my mouth is, I felt an obligation to put this book together. I felt a duty to pass on the knowledge I've gained through my experiences. I felt a responsibility to teach others the lessons I've learned, so I could spare them the need to learn those same lessons on their own. Because in the end, how can we expect those who follow in our footsteps to be more successful than we were if they have to learn the same lessons we did—on their own?

Anyone who has the responsibility for overseeing people must have adequate training in supervisory and management skills. *Supervisor, Manager, Leader: The Basics of Being a Boss* exists to help you first discover and then hone those skills. Supervisory skills are necessary for controlling and keeping employees within the parameters of the guiding documents of the organization, and management skills are necessary for controlling or managing the environment associated with those same people. Anytime you have one, you surely have the other. In other words, where you supervise people, you manage the environment associated with people; where you manage the environment associated with people, you surely have to supervise the people working within that environment.

Obviously, having the ability to supervise and manage is indispensable to anyone responsible for overseeing people. Any organization that promotes individuals to these positions must train their candidates ahead of time as well as provide ongoing training to those who are presently in those positions so they may both learn the concepts and become proficient at them. If the organization is foolish enough not to do this, then the individuals who aspire to these positions should take it upon themselves to seek out and learn these concepts on their own.

Is being a good supervisor and manager enough to "get by" in most organizations? The answer, unfortunately, is yes. However, I'd be willing to bet that those organizations are doing just that: getting by. But truly successful organizations—by which I mean those organizations that consistently and successfully meet their daily missions while clearly stating and pursuing their visions and then achieving those visions—are the organizations that have also trained and encouraged their supervisors and managers to be effective leaders.

Over the years, I have observed that successful organizations have not only taken the time and effort to teach and reinforce supervisory and management skills to their people but have also made it a point to teach and encourage those same supervisors and managers to be effective leaders. I believe that making this effort and investment in their people has, does, or will turn that organization around into one that is highly efficient, effective, and successful. The organization will also be one that has happier, more passionate, more satisfied, and more loyal employees who operate and perform as one team, not just as a group of individuals.

I realize that this certainly isn't the first book published on the subjects of supervision and management, and it clearly isn't the first book on leadership. But I believe it is different in that what I offer is neither theory nor philosophy. Rather, I present a compilation of simple, known concepts that have actually worked for me—those same simple, known concepts that most agencies, businesses, and organizations in general do a very poor job of teaching their employees to emulate. As a result, nothing is included in this book that I haven't learned many times on my own and usually the hard way —lessons I then applied in real life, to varying levels of success.

Don't get me wrong; I certainly encourage you to work toward advanced degrees in the subject matter of this book. I am a strong advocate of this. My goal in writing it, though, is to help you build a strong foundation from which you and your organization can operate so that you both become more successful.

Because this stuff isn't complicated, the layout of the book is purposely very easy to follow. There are three chapters: one on the supervisor, one on the manager, and one on the leader. The text is double-spaced to encourage you to take notes and highlight as you read. Each chapter ends with a workbook section where the main points of the chapter are reemphasized. The workbook is intended to give you the opportunity to become more self-aware of your effectiveness as you apply what you've learned and strive to improve in these specific areas.

It is important to understand that I do not think of myself as an expert on this particular subject matter. On the contrary, I consider myself a student. Again, these concepts are not new, and they are not mine. More importantly, they are all based on common sense. The problem has been that most of us were never taught these concepts. It has continually amazed me that more organizations haven't figured out that simply teaching their people basic supervision, management, and leadership concepts—the concepts I've included in this book—makes those same people much more effective and successful than those who work for organizations that leave it to chance.

This book is intended to help both up-and-coming and current supervisors and managers learn and improve in their positions. It is also intended to help you understand the importance of being a good leader who takes care of the people for whom you are responsible in either the public or private sector.

In my humble opinion, this book will help you in your professional growth. I believe there is always something new we can learn, whether in our chosen careers or in life itself. I believe it is my duty and responsibility to pass this information on to all of you. In return, I expect you to be a better supervisor, manager, and leader than I was. I also expect you to pass these lessons on to those who will follow in your footsteps.

Since the original writing of my book, I've had the privilege of being asked to present the material on site at many public- and private-sector organizations. Usually in the form of workshops, these opportunities to interact in person with those I attempt to reach with the written word have been extraordinarily rewarding. To actually see the light come on in the individual faces of those future and present bosses is a remarkable feeling. To receive calls or emails from individuals stating that what they learned actually helped them get promoted, or just become more effective in their present positions, not only reaffirms the validity of the book but gives me a feeling of satisfaction, knowing that I may have made the path to being an effective boss a little easier for someone.

My passion continues.

Chapter One: The Supervisor

Skills and Abilities of the Supervisor

Let's start with a simple definition for supervision: the act of overseeing, monitoring, and adjusting the activities and behavior of others. This is a blend of definitions I've read over the years that seems to best describe my view of the term. Supervisory skills are absolutely necessary when we're responsible for overseeing others in the workplace. People are the most important component of an effective and productive organization, whether in the public or private sector. So the focus here is keeping the employee between the lines, so to speak. Supervising people to ensure they are operating within the parameters of the guiding documents of the organization is critical. Are they meeting expectations? Are they adhering to the mission of the organization? Are they following the established behavioral guidelines? And when they aren't, are their supervisors doing their jobs and changing the negative behavior by coaching, counseling, and progressively disciplining them in order to get them back within the acceptable parameters of the organization?

In my experience, the two things that will help the supervisor the most are a solid knowledge of the organization's guiding documents and learning how to change negative behavior.

Guiding Documents

The glue that holds any organization together are the core values, mission statement, rules, policies, procedures, and guidelines of that organization. Supervising employees effectively is really not possible without a solid working knowledge of these guiding documents, which serve as the overriding umbrella under which the supervisor must keep the employees covered. In the best-case scenario, these guiding documents are visible and easily accessible to all employees. They are referred to and consulted upon when making decisions and used as justification for making those decisions. Most importantly, guiding documents must be acted upon and demonstrated on a regular basis by all bosses of the organization. When this is not the case, the supervisor's job is made much more difficult due to the fact that the organization doesn't appear to take its own guiding documents seriously.

Core Values

The core values of an organization are its heart and soul. They are (or should be) what guides the employees in how they treat their customers, how they treat other employees, and in their decision-making processes. In other words, the core values of a business form the basis of its organizational culture. Values such as honesty, courtesy, and respect are common core values. They are words that should not just hang in a framed document on the wall; they should be demonstrated in the everyday behavior of all employees. To ensure this occurs, the organization's supervisory personnel must be living examples and role models of these core values in action. In fact, if the supervisors truly live and demonstrate these core values, their people will take them to heart. In the long run, this will minimize the occurrences of negative behavior that the supervisor will have to deal with.

To me, an organization's values are the basis of its principles. During the fight for women's suffrage, Emmeline Pankhurst said, "Deeds, not words." Bosses can talk about values all day long, but if our subordinates don't see us demonstrating them on a regular basis, those values are only seen as words. An agency's principles are its core values in action. For ex-

22

ample, the core values of honesty and integrity can be translated into an operating principle such as "We will demonstrate honesty in all our interactions with both internal and external customers." The same can be done with the core values of courtesy and respect. For example: "The core values of courtesy and respect will be demonstrated, as well as prevail, in all interactions with both internal and external customers." In other words, if an agency's core values are regularly applied and reinforced as principles by the bosses, the subordinates will truly buy in to the fact that these values are more than just words. Eventually they become part of the organizational culture (values to principles to culture).

Mission Statements

Every organization has a mission or an expectation of what must be delivered to the customer on a daily basis. Most employees want to know what, how, and why they're doing what they're doing and how they fit into the organization's big picture. In other words, "What is our purpose," or "Why are we here?" In the public sector, this usually relates to what, how, and why services must be delivered to the citizen, taxpayer, or customer. In the private sector, the mission is related to what, how, and why the product or service is delivered to the buying customer, with the intent of that customer coming back to purchase the product or service again in the future. Without the daily mission of any organization being met, that organization will surely not be successful.

Equally important to the core values, the organization's mission must be more than just words in a frame on the wall; it must be kept in mind and referred to when making decisions at all levels of the organization.

Simply put, supervisors must have a sound understanding of the organizational mission. It is critical to the success of the organization that they keep themselves and the employees focused on accomplishing that very mission on a daily basis.

Performance Measures

Performance measures or benchmarks are realistic, measurable evaluation gauges put into place to ensure that the organizational or program performance stays on track and continues to meet the intent of the mission. They should be based upon applicable mandates or national or industry standards as opposed to being arbitrarily referenced. Performance measures or benchmarks are also a tool to be utilized by supervisors to improve individual or team performance. In addition, these measures can be used to justify to policy makers that the organization is either meeting the mission or needs increased revenue to improve operations in order to more effectively meet the mission.

During the Great Recession, I utilized our performance measures relating to industry-standard response times to educate our policy makers on what the results of reducing the number of staffed fire engines or ladder trucks would be. Subsequently, when the cuts were actually made, I had factual data to present to them as opposed to guesses or scare tactics on how those cuts might negatively affect the response times to our citizens.

Performance measures should not be used or even perceived as a way for supervisors to spy on or discipline employees. Benchmarks should be well understood and recognized throughout the organization. They must not only be evaluated on a regular basis but also the results must be shared with everyone in the company. Keeping employees informed of the status increases the buy-in and loyalty to the organization and encourages them to be part of the solution when adjustments or changes must be made to get the business back in line with the mission. If performance-measure results begin to show a need for the improvement of a certain individual, a confidential effort by the supervisor should be directed into a performance improvement plan, not a punitive improvement plan.

Vision Statement and Strategic Business Plan

A vision statement clarifies where the organization desires to go in the future. While it declares where the organization is going, it doesn't clarify how it will get there. That's where a strategic business plan comes in. The strategic business plan lays out how the organization will go about achieving its declared vision, step by step. These documents go (or should go) hand in hand. While all employees should be aware of them, the supervisor, manager, or leader must be very familiar with vision statement and strategic business plan because they are the ones who will guide and lead the organization through the process of realizing the organizational vision.

I will further clarify the importance of these two documents as they apply to "The Leader" chapter of the book.

Rules

There's no way around it: we live in a world of laws. So it's no secret that rules are—like it or not—a necessary element of every business. Rules are generally in place to control behavior. Everyone needs to be aware of them and abide by them. It's really that simple. They are a part of life, and without them we have chaos.

I also believe that you can't write a new rule every time a negative incident comes up. My view is that if the organization and its supervisors focused more on a value-based system as opposed to a rule-based system, employees would make the right decision more often, not because they don't want to get into trouble but because it's the right thing to do. As a result, the typical violations of the rules would be much less frequent. I am certainly not saying that we shouldn't have rules. We absolutely need basic rules in place. What I am saying is that if we blend a set of very basic rules with a culture of encouraging our people to make value- and principle-based decisions, it will increase the odds of good decisions being made. We do not live in a black-and-white world. On the contrary, our world is very gray. Rules alone cannot anticipate every situation our employees will encounter. They must be allowed to evaluate each issue they will face and make the right decision for that issue based upon the organizational core values and principles, not solely on hard-and-fast rules.

I believe the fire service in general—and my fire department specifically—is pretty good at this. It took time, but over the years it became quite normal to treat our customers and each other in ways that were based on the core values of the organization. Yes, we still had those individuals who would push the envelope. Yes, we still ended up having to change their behaviors, but when we compared the number of rule violations with the number of total employees, the percentage was very low. Again, this transition took quite some time in my fire department, and I certainly cannot take credit for it. The process started two fire chiefs before me, but I am certainly proud of the result.

Bottom line, supervisors must have a solid awareness of the organizational rules and be willing to implement a process to change negative behavior so they can keep the employees between the lines. I would also suggest focusing on organizational core values and principles to demonstrate to and teach employees to make the right decisions for the right reasons, not just to avoid discipline.

Policies, Procedures, and Guidelines

Not unlike rules and regulations, most organizations have policies and procedures. Policies are generally adopted or mandated ways of handling situations, and procedures are generally mandatory step-by-step ways of accomplishing tasks. Other organizations use guidelines. Guidelines are usually preferred ways of accomplishing tasks, with some discretion left to the employee from situation to situation. Whatever combination of policies, procedures, or guidelines a business or organization uses, the supervisor must obtain and sustain a working comprehension of these important guiding documents.

The critical thing that all supervisors need to remember is that policies, procedures, and guidelines must be realistic and reasonable. When one is found not to be so, the organization must adjust it until it is. Question how and why you do everything. If there is a better way to accomplish the task, try it out. If it doesn't work, all you've done is reinforce that the way you were accomplishing the task is still the best way.

Unfortunately, many supervisors believe that the answer to every problem or issue is to write a new policy or procedure. Is this easier than taking the time to find out what the root of the problem is? Is it easier than taking the time to discover that it may be a training or cultural issue that should be dealt with? Yes, of course it is, but it may not be the most effective way to prevent the problem from reoccurring in the future.

I myself fell into this trap while trying to save time on an issue that I misread. I should have gone to my people to gain their input before putting out the procedure. The issue itself is not important; what happened as a result of what I did is. Had I gone to my people for their input in the first place, I would have seen that issuing that new procedure at that time was not a good idea. In the end, because of the negative reaction to the procedure, and after considering the associated reasoning for the negative reaction, I cancelled the procedure. I went before the organization and apologized for not soliciting everyone's input first. By doing this, I not only learned a valuable lesson but also gained renewed respect from my people.

At times, there will be a need to pen a new policy or procedure. However, if you truly want the policy or procedure to be realistic and reasonable, you must understand the whole problem or issue. You can only do this by soliciting the input of those whom your solution will affect in the end. Everyone knows you have to solve the problem or issue, but by asking for his or her input—be it a new policy, procedure, or a change in training or culture— you gain buy-in from the very people your solution will affect. I would also recommend that even after preliminary input for a policy or procedure is received and considered, the organization should put the new document out as a draft for thirty days to allow for even more input. Additionally, all policies or procedures should be reviewed annually to ensure that they continue to be realistic and reasonable, and if found not to be, they should be updated or eliminated accordingly.

There are some policies that organizations will not have the ability to adjust. For example, those policies that are based upon state and federal law (e.g., discrimination, harassment, violence in the workplace, and substance abuse) will require mandated enforcement with little or no discretion left to the individual agencies or businesses.

Memorandum of Understanding

In the context of this book, a memorandum of understanding (MOU) relates to an agreed upon contract between the owners or entity of a business or organization and the organized labor group that represents the employees. These are very important documents of which a supervisor should have a good working understanding. Again, it's not necessary to memorize every line in the document, but the supervisor must be able to recognize issues that are regulated by the MOU. Labor/management MOUs are regulated by state and federal labor laws in regards to collective bargaining. Many times, MOUs are binding documents. Additionally, an MOU is a document negotiated in good faith and should be respected as such. Not taking the document seriously or ignoring the intent of it may result in governmental penalties or fines, is obviously not conducive to good business, and can seriously damage an organization's overall relationship with the employee group.

As a senior chief in my fire department, I made it a point to be aware of and understand the contents of the MOUs in place at the time. There was always a hard copy on my desk with highlighted marks, numerous notes, and tattered edges. I also maintained an open relationship with the current labor president. This was very beneficial in that we were able to discuss and strategize on any potential MOU-related issue and find a resolution before it became a problem. I could actually write another book on labor/management relations; suffice it to say for the purposes of this book that striving for a good labor/management relationship in your organization will pay numerous dividends down the road.

Changing Negative Behavior

As stated previously, while it is not necessary for supervisors to have all guiding documents memorized verbatim, they must know where to go to verify policy when a subordinate's behavior violates one of them. Arguably, the most important part of having this knowledge is recognizing when a perceived issue truly is an issue. If a supervisor cannot find a rule, regulation, policy, or procedure that is actually being violated by an employee, he or she must reconsider whether there even is an issue that must be dealt with at all.

If the guiding documents of an organization are developed collaboratively, instilled in and supported by all employees, reviewed and updated on a regular basis, and referenced continually by senior staff, the need for supervisors to actually enforce them through discipline will be a rare. In the perfect organization, the employees will take ownership of their own guiding documents and hold each other accountable to them.

The fact is, however, that there is no perfect organization, and the need to change negative behavior is a reality. As a result, when a supervisor determines that an employee is indeed acting outside of the guiding documents, she must have an idea of what to do next. While she can and should always consult with her peers, her supervisor, or the human resource department, the supervisor must have a solid understanding of the process for changing negative behavior, its intent, and its flexibility.

Expectations/Evaluations

Any hope of keeping employees within the guidelines of expected behavior starts with clear and realistic *expectations*. Does the organization have clear and realistic expectations for each position or rank? Are they current? Do they include the expectation of behaving and making decisions based on the core values and mission of the organization? Do the supervisors make these expectations clear to their subordinates initially and at least on an annual basis? And most importantly, are the employees evaluated annually on these clear and realistic expectations?

I worked for a few excellent supervisors—and many more who were not. Very few of them actually took the time to clearly articulate either the department's or their own expectations of me. Even when I was promoted to a new position, I had to research and interpret or guess what was now expected of me. As sad as this is, through my instruction and consulting experience since I've retired, I've found this clearly to be the norm in most organizations.

I preferred to schedule a specific time to sit down with each employee to review the expectations on which he was being evaluated for the previous year. I then explained my evaluation of his adherence to these expectations. I would allow him to ask any specific questions, followed by a mutual discussion on how I could help him improve and grow. Without a commitment from both of us, there truly was not much hope for improvement. However, as I discuss later, this was not our only meeting during the year, so there was really nothing on the evaluation of which the employee wasn't already aware. And this is key: if you're doing your job as a supervisor, you're continually meeting with the employee during the year as you mentor, coach, and counsel him. The employee should never be surprised by the content of the annual evaluation.

Mentoring

Whether an organization has a formal or informal mentoring program, the fact is, mentoring works. So what is a mentor? A mentor is a more senior or experienced employee who is tasked with supporting, teaching, and developing a less senior or experienced employee. A supervisor should, at the very least, be an informal mentor to those she supervises. Remember, the supervisor's job is to keep the employees operating within the parameters of the organization's guiding documents. So it only makes sense that she would want to develop employees the right way. This makes it easier in the long run, because employees will probably stay within those behavioral guidelines as a result of the mentoring. For the ultimate good of the company, developing those employees to be effective and productive team members now will likely ensure continued effectiveness and productivity into the future.

Is being a supervisor synonymous with being a mentor? While it should be, it's not. The average supervisor doesn't want to be inconvenienced by going the extra mile to support, teach, and develop their subordinates. That's really too bad, kind of ironic, or even stupid when you think about it. These types of supervisors are generally clueless to the fact that by not attempting to mentor their people, they're only making more work for themselves in the long run. The result of that lack of investment in the employees is a lack of investment by the employees. An unsupported employee will usually yield poor performance. This is quite probably due to the supervisor never being adequately trained for his position in the first place. As a result, he may not even realize his mistakes.

In addition to leading by example, a mentor takes the time to sit down with the new employee to initially make sure he understands the responsibilities associated with his position. Periodic and ongoing sit-down sessions are equally important to ensure that the employee develops confidence through proficiency in the position. In between these regular sit-down sessions, the mentor continually makes himself or herself available for any questions the employee may have about a specific situation or the position in general. By the way, a common byproduct of being a mentor to someone is becoming the best you can be at your own job.

Each of us can benefit from a mentor. If our bosses don't take their role as mentors seriously, we should look on our own for someone who does. The idea is to find someone we can learn from, emulate, and who can help us to develop professionally. We should seek out someone we can consult or just bounce ideas off when we're facing a dilemma. Remember, it will be nearly impossible to find an organization that teaches its employees every-thing they need to know for their respective positions, develops them, and prepares them for the next step in the promotional ladder.

Historically, my fire department—like most others at the time—would give a promotional exam for those interested in attaining the next highest po-sition in the chain of command. If the applicant did well enough on the exam, he would be promoted. There was no career development guide to follow and no promotional academy to attend prior to starting the new job. The fire chief would issue the new badge and say, "Good luck." This bothered me tremendously back then, but there was little I could do until I attained enough bugles on my uniform to effect some positive change, which I did. However, even with the addition of career development programs and promotional academies, there was a need for mentoring. It was simply impossible to teach individuals everything they needed to know about the job without someone with the experience and specific knowledge of the position round-ing off the edges and coloring in the gray areas for the newly promoted indi-vidual. We all need that mentor to fill in the gaps, to help us be the best we can be at our jobs, and to help us prepare for whatever is next.

Coaching or Counseling

No one is perfect. We all need to be reminded from time to time of what our daily mission is; what is expected of us; how we should be performing; or what the rules, policies, procedures, and guidelines are. If supervisors are doing their jobs, they're regularly coaching and counseling their employees to keep them within the parameters of the organizational guiding documents.

In general, coaching is used when employees are struggling with a performance-related issue, and counseling is used when employees are struggling with a behavior- or rule-related issue. Both require the supervisor to care enough to address the issue with the employee, and both require a commitment from the supervisor to help the employee.

In the vast majority of incidences, I found that when I addressed these issues while they were still minor, I rarely had to address them again. If a supervisor doesn't take the time or make the effort to use coaching/counseling as tools, she's not performing as an effective supervisor. Why would I want to ignore the issue now? In doing so, I'm going to be forced to expend much more effort and probably heartache when I have to discipline the employee because the once-minor issue has now grown into a major one. Again, this is more than likely due to the supervisor not being adequately trained for the position.

I supervised a fire captain years ago who was a hard worker and very good at what he did on the emergency scene; however, he was slow to coach or counsel his people when needed. As a result, small issues unnecessarily became larger issues, which he was then forced to deal with but at a more labor-intensive level. When I counseled him on this, he stated to me that he didn't like conflict. My comment to him was, "No one likes conflict, but it's part of your job as a supervisor, so get over it." Though no one really enjoys conflict, as a supervisor, conflict is—in one form or another—almost always present and must be dealt with.

Just to clarify, coaching or counseling doesn't have to feel like—and actually shouldn't feel like—a scolding or admonishment to the employee.

The first coaching or counseling session is simply that: a coaching or counseling moment. To illustrate, as a battalion chief I had to counsel a captain for a behavioral issue. I can't remember what the issue was, but I do remember very clearly his reply to me as we parted. He simply said, "Thank you, boss. That was the nicest ass-chewing I've ever received." And guess what? I never had another issue with that captain.

Conflict Resolution

When most people think of conflict, they think of something that is a threat or something that should be avoided. For much of my life I shared this feeling. However, over the years, and through my own life, work, and especially supervisor experience, I've learned to look at conflict as more of an opportunity than a threat. It's an opportunity to resolve the conflict and, as a result, make the individuals and organizations involved stronger and smarter for having gone through the resolution process.

Avoiding or ignoring conflict is not a good practice. Unfortunately, supervisors often choose to do this because it is the easiest choice in the short term. "Let's just ignore the issue or conflict for now because we don't want to or don't have time to deal with it." Almost always, choosing this option will guarantee that the issue will resurface at a later time, often as an even larger conflict than it was originally.

I've found that the most important thing to keep in mind when dealing with conflict is the organization's core values. Remember, the core values are intended to guide us when dealing with both internal and external customers. If we do this, we really can't go wrong. Core values such as honesty, courtesy, and integrity will help us deal with conflict, whether the conflict is with our internal customers (subordinates), between our subordinates, with our superiors, or with an external customer or element.

The first step is to get both parties—individuals or groups—to sit down and clarify the conflict or issue. Misperceptions that lead to misunderstandings often are the cause of conflict. Years ago I had a fire chief who used to say, "Perception is reality to those who are watching us." This was one of the most important things I learned as a future boss. Once an issue is clarified, we may find out that in some situations our perceptions were totally wrong and that there really was no conflict: problem solved. I observed this several times as a supervisor. But if we don't sit down under the umbrella of our core values, we may never even realize this—and the misguided conflict will continue unnecessarily.

If, after clarifying the issue, we find that we do have a legitimate conflict, the parties must work through the resolution process. The goal of the process is for the parties to initiate their own possible solutions, actively discuss the merits, then agree to move forward while embracing the agreed upon resolution(s). I found that, as the boss in the room, it was important that I keep the clarified conflict or issue in the forefront by writing it down and keeping the parties on track, and to not allow the discussion to deviate. It was also important for me to facilitate the process without micromanaging it. While I would need to approve the end result, it was critical that I allowed the parties to move through the process of their own volition. If the supervisor micromanages the resolution process without simply facilitating it, the parties may not totally buy in to the end resolution, believing it was the supervisor's process, not their own.

In my experience, the conflict-resolution process may evolve or develop through several phases. It may start out as a competition between parties with both sides unwilling to relent. If facilitated effectively and if the discussion is kept professional and respectful, I found that many times the competition turned into compromise, with both parties realizing that the give-and-take process was less stressful than competing. Other times, I'd see the competition evolve into collaboration, with both parties working together to find an acceptable resolution, or both suddenly realizing they actually had the same goal.

Amazingly enough, if all parties kept an open mind, once in a while one side would decide that the other party did indeed have valid points and would actually relent to the opposing position. Or, one party would decide that the issue was just not worth the effort it was going to take to compete. I've done this personally many times after asking myself a question I learned from another former fire chief of mine: "Is this a hill worth dying on?" Kind of puts things in perspective, doesn't it?

To summarize, a supervisor should look at conflict as an opportunity, not a threat. She should get the parties together and clarify the issue. She should facilitate—not micromanage—a professional, respectful process that allows both parties to work through the issue to an acceptable resolution, keeping the core values of the company in the forefront of all discussions and decisions. Remember that "perception is reality to those who are observing us," and don't be afraid to ask yourself, "Is this a hill worth dying on?"

Progressive Discipline

Unless the issue is an acute violation severe enough to warrant an immediate investigation and possibly discipline, the vast majority of personnel issues can be handled through the normal process of coaching or counseling the employee, in conjunction with effective usage of the expectation/evaluation system. In fact, I prefer not to use the term "discipline" at all. I look at the whole process as "changing negative behavior." After all, isn't this the intent of the whole process? Wouldn't you rather help this employee—on whom, by the way, your organization has spent a vast amount of money in wages, benefits, and training—change his or her negative behavior and get back on the path of productivity, rather than immediately focusing on disciplining him or her?

Keep in mind that actually disciplining an employee usually includes taking something from him such as pay, rank, position, or the job itself (also known as property rights in the public sector), and such actions may leave the employee with a poor attitude toward the supervisor and the organization.

That's not to say that those issues won't arise that can only be handled through discipline, but the vast majority of issues can be handled successfully when the supervisor recognizes an issue, coaches or counsels the employee right away, and uses the regular written expectation/evaluation process effectively.

And when those few-and-far-between issues emerge that cannot be handled within the coaching, counseling, and written expectation/evaluation process, the supervisor must be familiar with what is next. In general, one must know what the progressive-discipline process includes. This process begins at the lowest level, such as time off without pay, and leads up to something much more painful, such as demotion or termination from employment. While disciplining an employee may be painful, we need to keep in mind that this employee is still one of our people and that the discipline is not punitive but a continuing attempt to change the negative behavior. There were many sleepless nights and more than a few tears associated with my issuing severe discipline to my people. It was clearly not the best part of my job, but it was necessary nonetheless.

It should go without saying, but I shall say it: I want to emphasize the importance of adhering to due process for the employee (which is usually derived from state and federal law) and giving them the benefit of the doubt until a fair and thorough investigation proves otherwise. I would be less than truthful if I said giving them the benefit of the doubt was easy. There were times during my tenure as a senior chief officer when there were parallel investigations—one administrative within the department and the other criminal—being conducted by law enforcement and the district attorney. Not rushing to judgement was difficult, but it was absolutely critical that I remained neutral on the matter. We must remember that these are our people; they are not the enemy. We must always resist the temptation to prejudge and always adhere to due process in accordance with applicable labor laws and memorandums of understanding.

Your human resources department personnel should be instructing new supervisors as well as continually educating veteran supervisors on this process. If they are not, you should ask them to do so. It is simply wrong to place this awesome responsibility upon a new supervisor without adequate training.

Supervisors must realize that it's not a matter of if they will be dealing with some form of personnel-related issues, but when. The higher one advances in an organization, the more frequently he or she will have to play a role in the process of changing negative behavior. I never believed that I would be dealing with issues related to alcohol and substance abuse, arrests and criminal charges, violence in the workplace, sexual harassment, marriage and relationships, spousal abuse, theft, sick leave abuse, excessive sick leave usage, and poor performance, but I did.

So whether you are a new supervisor or an or have been supervising for many years, make sure you are familiar with the guiding documents of your organization, especially in the area of core values, mission, rules, policies, procedures, and guidelines, as well as how to change negative behavior effectively through coaching, counseling, evaluating, and issuing progressive discipline while following due process. By doing so, your life as a supervisor will become much less stressful.

Workbook for Supervisors

Guiding Documents

Do I have a working knowledge of the guiding documents of my organization?

_____

_____

Can I list them?

_____

_____

How can I improve?

_____

_____

_____

_____

_____

_____

_____

_____

_____

_____

_____

_____

_____

What are my organization's core values?

_____

_____

Do I understand the importance of keeping them in mind at all times as a supervisor?

_____

_____

Do I understand the importance of demonstrating and instilling these core values in my people?

_____

_____

Do I understand that my organization's core values are the foundation of its culture?

_____

_____

How can I improve?

_____

_____

_____

_____

_____

What is the mission of my organization?

_____

_____

Do I understand the importance of keeping it in mind as I perform my duties as a supervisor?

_____

_____

Do I articulate to my people where they fit within the mission?

_____

_____

How can I improve?

_____

_____

_____

_____

_____

_____

_____

_____

_____

_____

_____

_____

Am I aware of and do I monitor the results of the performance measures related to my area of responsibility?

_____

_____

Are these performance measures realistic and measurable?

_____

_____

Do I take necessary action to make adjustments in reference to the results?

_____

_____

How can I improve?

_____

_____

_____

_____

_____

_____

_____

_____

_____

_____

_____

Do I have a good working knowledge of my organization's rules and regulations?

_____

_____

Do I understand the advantages of emphasizing the organization's core values and their connections with employee behavior?

_____

_____

How can I improve?

_____

_____

_____

_____

_____

_____

_____

_____

_____

_____

_____

_____

_____

_____

_____

Do I have a good working knowledge of my organization's policies, procedures, and guidelines?

_____

_____

Are they realistic and currently necessary?

_____

_____

How can I improve?

_____

_____

_____

_____

_____

_____

_____

_____

_____

_____

_____

_____

_____

_____

_____

_____

_____

Do I have a good working knowledge of the current labor/management MOU(s) in my organization?

_____

_____

How can I improve?

_____

_____

_____

_____

_____

_____

_____

_____

_____

_____

_____

_____

_____

_____

_____

_____

_____

_____

_____

Changing Negative Behavior

Do I understand my organization's process for changing negative behavior, including progressive discipline and due process?

_____

_____

And, most importantly, do I understand my role as a supervisor within this process?

_____

_____

How can I improve?

_____

_____

_____

_____

_____

_____

_____

_____

_____

_____

_____

Do I clearly convey to my employees the organizational expectations they are expected to accomplish?

_____

_____

Do I also clearly convey the expectations I have for them?

_____

_____

Do my expectations for them support the organization's expectations?

_____

_____

Do I do this on an annual basis at minimum?

_____

_____

How can I improve?

_____

_____

_____

_____

_____

_____

_____

Do I consistently mentor my people with the intent of helping them be the best they can be in their present positions?

_____

_____

Do I regularly schedule time with them?

_____

_____

Am I helping them overcome their weaknesses and build on their strengths?

_____

_____

Am I preparing them for the next promotional step?

_____

_____

How can I improve?

_____

_____

_____

_____

_____

_____

_____

_____

Do I coach or counsel my people when necessary and without procrastination to help them stay within the expectations and parameters of the organizational guiding documents?

_____

_____

How can I improve?

_____

_____

_____

_____

_____

_____

_____

_____

_____

_____

_____

_____

_____

_____

_____

_____

Do I issue timely, thorough evaluations?

_____

_____

_____

_____

Do I make efforts to provide ongoing feedback to my people so that there are no surprises during evaluations?

_____

_____

_____

_____

_____

Are these evaluations a logical follow-up to the mentoring, coaching, and counseling I've done with them throughout the year?

_____

_____

_____

_____

How can I improve?

_____

_____

_____

_____

Do I understand the intent of progressive discipline within the parameters of changing negative behavior?

_____

_____

Do I understand my organization's process for progressive discipline and my role in it as a supervisor?

_____

_____

How can I improve?

_____

_____

_____

_____

_____

_____

_____

_____

_____

_____

_____

_____

_____

_____

Do I understand that conflict should be looked upon as an opportunity to re-solve issues and, as a result, make my employees and the organization stronger for having gone through the process of resolution?

_____

_____

_____

Do I recognize the importance of not ignoring conflict?

_____

_____

_____

Do I understand the importance of clarifying the issue, then facilitating the resolution process without micromanaging it?

_____

_____

_____

Do I understand the importance of keeping our core values in mind when dealing with conflict?

_____

_____

_____

_____

How can I improve?

_____

_____

_____

_____

_____

_____

_____

_____

_____

_____

_____

_____

_____

_____

Do I understand that my organization has a huge investment in its people?

_____

_____

Do I keep this in mind as I perform my supervisory responsibilities?

_____

_____

How can I improve?

Do I keep in mind that these are my people I am supervising?

_____

_____

Do I believe they deserve my very best as their supervisor?

_____

_____

How can I improve?

_____

_____

_____

_____

_____

_____

_____

_____

_____

_____

_____

_____

_____

_____

_____

_____

Chapter Two: The Manager

Skills and Abilities of the Manager

My definition of management is the act of controlling, monitoring, and adjusting the "things" associated with your people and the environment they operate in. The focus here is overseeing *things*, rather than *people*. Managing things is just as important as supervising people.

When you're managing things there are people involved, not only those you're supervising but also yourself. With this being the case, the first things we'll talk about managing are responsibilities and time. If we can't manage our own responsibilities and our time, how will we be able to manage other things such as programs, special projects, budgets, committees, conflict, and change?

Managing Responsibilities

I never aspired to be a fire chief. I ended up in the position through unforeseen events. I stepped up when asked, but I really didn't know what I was responsible for. Yes, I observed the fire chief position from the number-two spot in the chain of command, but I was normally focused on my own responsibilities as a division chief. So when I found myself in this new position, I had to conduct some very rapid research to learn what I was actually responsible for.

If someone were to ask you what you as a manager are responsible for in your present job, would you be able to respond accurately? Do you really even know? If you don't know, don't you think you should? Or maybe you're content with simply watching others in your position and assuming they know the job responsibilities. If you don't know what your responsibilities are, how do you know if you're effectively managing them? Where would you even go to find the legitimate answers to these questions?

The first place you should look is your job description. This document (one I'm guessing you probably haven't looked at since you took the position, am I right?) will detail exactly what your positional responsibilities are. Print a copy, read it, ask your boss clarifying questions, then keep it somewhere where you have to look at it periodically. Once you truly understand what your responsibilities are in your present position, you can start to better manage them.

After your job description, the next place you should look to clarify your responsibilities are the written "expectations" associated with your organization's personnel evaluation system, as we discussed in the previous chapter on supervision. If you receive an annual evaluation from your immediate supervisor, he or she is evaluating your compliance with the stated expectations of your position. These should be very closely aligned with your position's job description, but they should be more detailed to allow your supervisor to evaluate at the level at which you are complying.

Finally, simply ask your supervisor if there are any additional expectations he or she has of you. Just as you may have with those you supervise, your supervisor may have some additional expectations of you. These additional expectations are probably not written down but are important to your boss. As long as they don't conflict with the organizational expectations of your position, you need to comply with them as well. Just as with your job description, keep your job expectations handy for periodic review and self-evaluation.

Now that you understand what things you are responsible for managing, let's make sure you have the time to manage them.

Managing Time

I love this quote on time management from Michael Altshuler: "The bad news is time flies. The good news is you're the pilot." We've all had those days where we've wondered where the day went and why we didn't get anything accomplished. While we certainly can't predict the occasional surprise or derailment to our daily routine, the real culprit of those nonproductive days is almost always ourselves. Managing your time is a huge part of being successful, both personally and professionally.

Time management was—and still is—one of my biggest challenges. It's impossible to know how much good was left undone by allowing myself to get pulled in different directions. While I thought I was doing the right thing at the time, I look back and wonder how much more I could have accomplished if I'd been a better time manager. I was constantly trying to improve in this area, and I did. I just never improved to the point that I felt I was as effective as I could have been. I didn't then—and don't now—have a clever system or easy-to-remember acronym for time management. I do have real-life experience that has taught me several concepts that I'll share with you.

Post a List of Responsibilities

As I already discussed, you must first be aware of your responsibilities. Once you have that awareness, I recommend making a list of those responsibilities. Place the list on your desk, or as I did, on the bulletin board in front of my desk (or any location that is "in your face" for most of your day). I also had a handwritten note next to my responsibility list that simply said, "Should you be doing this?" In other words, is what you're doing at this second actually one of your responsibilities? This responsibility list will be your foundation for your time management. As you brainstorm about projects you'd like to start or take part in, as you decide what committees to form or join, as you decide what meetings you should attend, and ultimately, what entries you decide to make in your calendar, make sure that they are consistent with the responsibilities on your list.

Now, obviously, we all have bosses, and whether we like it or not, there are some projects, meetings, or events that we're just going to have to accept or attend, even if they aren't associated with the responsibilities on our list. That's life, and there's really nothing we can do about that. But we must commit to controlling those time-eating calendar entries when we can.

Prioritize Your Schedule Each Day

No matter how good you are at keeping your calendar in line with your responsibilities, you must reevaluate and prioritize at the beginning of each day. Distractions and emergencies are a fact of life, and it is unrealistic to believe that they can be avoided completely. However, make sure that those distractions and perceived emergencies are actually legitimate interruptions to your day before you start rearranging your priority list. Take a look at your schedule, and then fold in the distractions and last-minute emergencies. Inevitably, this will require you to reevaluate what you can realistically accomplish during the day. Yes, I said *realistically*. You can only do so much in one day, and you want the results at the end of the day to be quality results related to your responsibilities.

When I was first assigned to an administrative position, I mistakenly believed I could take one project at a time, research it, develop it, implement it, and then move on to the next project. Boy, was I mistaken. In the first week, I learned that daily distractions are the norm rather than the exception. As a result, I learned in a hurry to be realistic as to what I could actually expect to accomplish. So be sure to remain flexible when reevaluating your calendar and daily schedule. After this daily reevaluation process, simply prioritize your items. Yes, some items may need to be postponed, but that's why we prioritize, isn't it? Whatever is left undone at the end of the day will get reevaluated the next morning against the calendar and associated distractions and emergencies of that day. That's reality.

During my tenure as fire chief, I had two high-profile, ulcer-causing (literally) responsibilities that demanded the vast majority of my time: managing a shrinking budget during the recession and dealing with the politics of regionalizing three fire agencies into one. Each of these tasks truly required full-time attention. While it may have been required, it simple was not possible. Despite working twelve-hour days and weekends and delegating what I could, there was no way I was going to be able give each of these responsibilities the attention they needed without daily prioritization of the current issues. This principle is sound whether you're a fire chief, a CEO, or a first-level supervisor.

Over the years, I also learned to take full advantage of the electronic calendar. I found that by regularly marking out time in the day for things such as returning emails and voice mails, visiting with and checking on the welfare of my people, and—imagine this—quiet office time, I was able to actually get something accomplished. I also found that by marking time out for these things in the same time slot each day, my bosses, peers, and assistants became familiar with my schedule and generally didn't try to interfere with my routine.

One of the most important practices I established and continued throughout my tenure as fire chief was having my assistant schedule me at a different fire station once a week to have lunch with my firefighters. Did I really have time to do this? No, I didn't. However, as you'll read later in the book, that relationship was critical to the success of the department. During these extremely difficult times, they needed me, and I definitely needed them to continue to deliver our mission to the citizens. In other words, I made this a personal priority, even though it wasn't listed in any document as one of my responsibilities.

Delegate Properly

One person can only accomplish so much. As a result, if we don't delegate, we're not maximizing the potential of our organizations. Delegation is an extremely valuable tool—when properly used. There are several benefits to the concept, including but not limited to more efficient time management; development of our people; and increased utilization of our people's ingenuity, innovation, and creativity. But in order to realize these benefits, we must use delegation properly.

We can start by making sure that whatever we are delegating is, in fact, our responsibility to delegate in the first place. In other words, make sure the project or job is yours to delegate and that it fits within your list of responsibilities. If it doesn't, you probably shouldn't be dealing with it at all, and most certainly you should not be delegating it.

When you delegate, make sure you give clear parameters to your subordinates. What are the expectations? What are you actually asking them to do? What is the budget? What is the time frame? How often do you want to be updated on the status? How much leeway do they have in the way of innovation, ingenuity, and creativity? If you don't set clear expectations and parameters, you will end up using more time and effort in correcting a poor result or in frustration doing the project or job yourself. And worse yet, you'll inadvertently frustrate or discourage the person to whom you delegated the project.

Pick the right person for the project or delegation. Do they have the ability to complete the task? Do they have the time? And if they don't, can you as the manager make arrangements to give them the time they need?

Monitor the process, but don't micromanage the employee. We've all experienced this from a boss. If you really feel the need to control the process that much, you probably did a poor job in explaining the expectations to the person, or you picked the wrong person for the job in the first place. Either way, it's your fault. Lighten up and trust your people. If the project or job doesn't have to be done exactly one way, back off and let them use their individual talents and abilities. If you can't trust your people to do the job, you probably haven't developed them as you should have. Again, this is your fault, not theirs.

It's also important to remember not to overload your people with delegated assignments. Be aware of their workloads. They're probably good employees in the first place, or you wouldn't have trusted them enough to delegate work to them. This means they probably won't want to tell you when they're overloaded because they don't want to disappoint you. This is all the more reason for you to be aware of their workloads and not take advantage of their work ethic. To this point, remember that spreading delegation around to other employees, not just your go-to producers, gives them a chance to be challenged and to develop as well, but most importantly, to also feel that you have confidence in them to do the job. Finally, when the task is completed, give your people the credit for a job well done. This should go without saying, but unfortunately it can't. I'll discuss this more later.

Managing Programs

My definition of a program is a planned, coordinated group of responsibilities, controlled by policies and procedures, and designed to meet a specific mission. In the fire service, for example, we have fire-prevention programs, fire-education programs, fire-training programs, and fire-suppression programs, to name a few. Each of these programs must be directed, monitored, and adjusted by a manager.

Earlier in the book, I discussed the importance of the organizational mission. It may seem overly simplistic, but also giving every program its own mission statement or statement of purpose will help tremendously in keeping that program on track. Doing this will help the program stay true to its original intent and help the manager more efficiently monitor and evaluate the performance of the program over time. If it becomes difficult to develop a mission or purpose for a program, you should ask yourself, "Is this program even relevant or necessary, or are we just wasting our time and money on a program simply because we've always had it?" Think about it.

Also, as discussed earlier in the book, one of the best methods of monitoring a program is to establish and regularly evaluate the results of performance measures. Performance measures are derived from national or industry standards as well as from the organizational or program mission. They are written as measurable goals that are easily read (i.e., they don't contain a lot of jargon or hard-to-understand language). The data is continually collected and analyzed to give the program manager a snapshot of how effectively the program is performing. When the results are not as expected, the manager must make adjustments when possible or advise the policy makers of the issue.

Managing Special Projects

For the purposes of this book, let's define a "special project" as a temporary assembly of employees to solve a specific problem or develop a solution for a particular issue. Every organization has them, and they all need to be managed properly. If they are not properly managed, time is wasted, the problem or issue continues, and both productivity and morale suffer.

The manager must be clear as to what the special project is. What is the problem that must be overcome? What is the budget for the project? What is expected in the way of status reports and deadlines? Who is in charge? Again, just as I stated above in regards to managing programs, the manager must be strong enough to ask if this special project is actually necessary and what other work may need to be put aside to focus on its completion. Additionally, as mentioned before, it is important for managers to pay attention to their people's workloads. Consistently putting extra work on the same employees because they are top performers may burn them out.

After setting the special project participants up for success, the manager must stand back, empower her people, and let them go. The balancing act is to then monitor the progress without micromanaging. The trick here is to monitor the progress of the group and interject information necessary to keep the special project on track and pointed in the right direction—without interfering with the creative flow of the group or the empowerment and development of the individuals.

The manager must keep an open mind as to what the final solution or recommendation may be. If he can't do this, he may as well do the project himself. But if he can keep an open mind and is willing to consider results different from those he may come up with, he will not only increase the odds of obtaining creative solutions but also indirectly develop his people in the process.

The biggest special project I was involved with as fire chief was the merging of my city fire department with the county fire department and a contiguous fire district. This was a huge project that involved all aspects of the organization. It also demanded a very large portion of my time. While this process helped me grow immensely as a manager in the areas of time management, delegation, empowerment, and keeping an open mind, it came at a personal cost physically, mentally, and emotionally. If you are interested in learning more about this special project, take a look at my book, <u>Regionalizing Fire Service Delivery Systems</u>.

Managing Budgets

My time as fire chief coincided with the worst years of the Great Recession. As a result, I learned firsthand the importance of being able to financially support the services delivered by the organization. My budget was significantly reduced from fiscal year to fiscal year, sometimes even in the middle of those fiscal years. During that time, I continued hearing from the policy makers that I was expected to do more with less. After evaluating and reevaluating my department's priorities, I learned that this was simply not going to be possible. If we were going to be able to continue to meet our core mission and deliver the best emergency services possible to our citizens, while at the same time supporting and keeping my people safe while they delivered those services, something had to give. The budget simply wasn't going to allow us to do "more with less." We were going to have to do "less with less" and only concentrate on delivering priority services and supporting the employees who were delivering those services.

Out of frustration, at a weekly city manager/department director meeting, I announced that the fire department was reevaluating our priorities in anticipation of having to begin operating with the "less with less" mentality. While the city manager wasn't pleased with my catching him off guard with the announcement, and rightfully so (I knew my timing was off by reading his face), he did see the logic in it, as did the other department directors. It was a realization for all of us that we were in extraordinary economic times, and we simply could not continue operating as we had in the past.

I wish I could tell you that I received sufficient training to effectively manage a budget as I was promoted in my organization, but sadly, I cannot. Other than what I observed and absorbed through watching my former bosses, there was no formal public-sector budgeting education. Had I not made the effort on my own to seek out financial professionals to learn all I could, I quite probably would have made some very costly mistakes. Again, we see the unfortunate pattern of organizations not preparing their people for success as they are promoted.

Managing budgets is clearly an important part of both public- and private-sector organizations. However, in the public sector, we're talking about the budgeting of taxpayer dollars. As a result, we have an obligation to be good stewards of those dollars. We can never forget this critical aspect of public-sector budgeting.

The budgeting process of an organization is ongoing. Simply, it begins with projecting the revenue and anticipating the needs of the upcoming fiscal year. As a manager, in addition to having a current strategic business plan to assist you, it is very important to include your people in the budgeting process. They are the best source for keeping you informed as to what their current and future needs are in order to perform their jobs effectively. Additionally, by including your people in the budgeting process, you teach them the "why we budget the way we budget" information they should be aware of. Once the budget year begins, the process of constantly monitoring and adjusting the current budget is never ending. Before we know it, we're starting the budgeting cycle over again and beginning to anticipate the revenue and the needed expenditures for the next fiscal year.

For public-sector accounting and reporting, the standard is the Governmental Accounting Standards Board (GASB; http://www.gasb.org/home). According to the GASB's website:

> The GASB's mission is to establish standards for financial reporting that provide decision-useful information to assist individuals in assessing a government's financial condition and performance. Today, taxpayers, holders of municipal bonds, members of citizen groups, legislators and oversight bodies rely on this financial information to shape public policy and make investments. These standards also help government officials demonstrate to their constituents their accountability and stewardship over public resources.

Because my budget-management experience was in the public sector, I won't attempt to get into the specifics of private-sector budgeting. I will, however, state that for private-sector budgetary accounting and reporting, the standard is put forth by the Financial Accounting Standards Board (FASB; http://www.fasb.org/home). According to the FASB website:

> The mission of the FASB is to establish and improve standards of financial accounting and reporting that foster financial reporting by nongovernmental entities that provides decision-useful information to investors and other users of financial reports. That mission is accomplished through a comprehensive and independent process that encourages broad participation, objectively considers all stakeholder views, and is subject to over-

sight by the Financial Accounting Foundation's Board of Trustees.

Whether you operate in the public or private sector, if you haven't received training on overseeing a budget or you're uncomfortable with how to manage a budget, the secret is to get help right away. Don't be afraid to ask questions. Basic budgeting is really not that difficult with the proper training and mentoring. Hopefully your company has given you the necessary training, but if that isn't the case, at the very least, find an effective mentor and learn all you can from him or her. Most importantly, don't perpetuate the problem. After you are comfortable with the budgeting process, see that the employees you're responsible for get the training they need for their current and future positions.

Make sure everyone who has the authority to access your budget understands what the parameters and limitations are for them. Additionally, understand that you must get frequent reports on the status of how your budget is doing. Weekly or monthly meetings reviewing these reports with your budget team are not too frequent. Are we on track for projected revenues and anticipated expenditures? Are we seeing any possible negative trends that we must deal with immediately? If so, we must have the courage to step up and make any necessary adjustments. Waiting and hoping the situation will improve on its own is not realistic and certainly not wise.

Make sure that you keep your bosses and your subordinates up to date on the status of your budget. There can be no surprises: good or bad, you must keep them both advised.

Managing Committees

One of the first things I did after becoming fire chief was to evaluate each department committee and its status. Those that didn't have a current mission or purpose or those that were no longer productive were eliminated. Many public-sector organizations, including my own at the time, become used to the status quo of having committees and related committee meetings, even when those committees no longer have a purpose, have become unproductive, or are no longer effective. In the private sector this doesn't usually occur because managers are constantly evaluating the purpose, the productivity, and the effectiveness of committees. Time is money, and wasting time on unnecessary committees will eventually be detrimental to a business's bottom line. We need to get better at this in the public sector. Remember, our citizens are trusting us with their hard-earned tax dollars.

Committees are usually established for the purpose of making recommendations to the individual or body of individuals who have the decision-making responsibility for the organization. The committee may be made up of subject-matter experts or a cross section of individuals with a diverse views and experiences who have been purposely placed together to increase the odds of the boss making the best decision for the company.

As far as the ideal size of a committee, generally speaking, a group numbering from seven to ten individuals is most effective. These numbers usually give the group an adequate diversity of opinion without being so large that it becomes too cumbersome and slow to produce the needed recommendations or results.

As alluded to earlier, one of the biggest time wasters in any organization is unnecessary and unproductive meetings. First, make sure every committee is actually necessary. If the committee is necessary, ensure that there is a clear mission attached to it. It's also important to determine if the committee serves a temporary or permanent purpose.

Once the committee is deemed necessary, make sure each associated meeting is necessary. Individuals in your organization are busy, and they don't have time to attend unnecessary meetings. If there is information that needs to be shared, consider utilizing email. If there are decisions that must be made, be sure to have an agenda made up prior to the meeting, and then make sure you stick to it. It's important to get the agenda out in advance, so all participants can have sufficient time to review or research prior to the meeting.

During the committee meeting (or any meeting, for that matter) eliminate distractions, handle the formalities, state the issue(s), allow constructive discussion within the time constraints, and then make a decision. If the decision turns out to be one that must be readdressed later, that's fine, but remember that far too many meetings go on and on with unproductive and unrelated discussion and, as a result, no decision on the issue is ever reached. If you achieve timely results from each meeting in reference to organizational issues, you'll get far more respect as a manager, and the organization will be far more productive in the long run.

Sharing the minutes of committee meetings—or again, any meeting—with the rest of the organization is critical to establishing and building support for the mission of the committee. Unless there is a good reason to delay sharing this information (which should almost never happen), prompt distribution of the minutes should occur after each committee meeting. Secrecy and lack of transparency, or even the perception of such, will quickly result in widespread lack of support for the committee.

Managing Conflict

Earlier in the book, I talked about how a supervisor needs the ability to apply the skill of conflict resolution when dealing with the people of an organization. Allowing unresolved, destructive conflict to exist in any business is not productive. However, when used in a constructive manner—when it is controlled and utilized to gain different points of view while attempting to come up with the best solution to a problem—conflict can actually be productive. The manager who utilizes the diversity of the workforce to ultimately help him make the final decision on an issue is the manager who understands that he can't possibly have all the answers, keeps an open mind, and trusts his people—and he will make the right decision a high percentage of the time.

The concept of constructive conflict is simple; effectively carrying it out, however, is not. When you need the best solution possible to solve a significant problem or improve a situation, a healthy, passionate debate is needed to truly vet the options. This concept is very effective in working committees. Committee members, even if their suggested solution or recommendation is not ultimately selected, appreciate that their voice is being heard and their ideas are being considered and debated. Because of this appreciation, they will more than likely support and buy in to the final decision. By the way, in my experience, regularly utilizing this process builds stronger team cohesion in the workplace.

However, it is important for the manager to remember that everyone must be aware of the ground rules in a constructive-conflict session before the session begins. Everyone must understand the concept of constructive-conflict sessions and their advantages to the organization. Mutual respect for each individual's position and maintaining open minds must prevail. Everyone must understand the specific issue up for discussion, and the session must have a time limit placed on it. It is also important that the manager has the ability to sense and mitigate the emotions of the individual members during the debate session. Because of the real risk of a meeting turning destructive instead of constructive if not controlled properly, a manager must be comfortable with utilizing this concept and should probably observe how it is done a few times before attempting to use it. Keep in mind that the intent of constructive debate is to encourage members to voice and actively debate all points of view, with the intended result of reaching the best decision for the organization. Passion is good, but losing control of emotions is not and will lead to a destructive-conflict session and hurt feelings.

In my first experience with constructive conflict, I was impressed that the boss allowed us to passionately voice and defend our opinions. However, he didn't really place any parameters on the session. So after thirty minutes or so of passionate debate, I found myself yelling at him. I had lost perspective of the issue and had let my emotions and ego take over. What started out as a constructive session on an issue turned into a destructive yelling match that I angrily marched out of, leaving the issue unresolved. Now, I am not ashamed of passionately debating the issue. I was—and still am— ashamed of losing control of my emotions and professional demeanor in an environment that included subordinates. In other words, I blew it. I humbly apologized to him later in the day and he graciously allowed me to keep my job. To his credit he continued allowing us to use the constructive-conflict concept, ultimately resulting in our ability to hold lively, passionate, productive meetings that almost always resulted in sound, well-debated decisions.

Managing Change

Arguably one of the most important skills for a manager to possess is that of managing change. Change must and will occur; it's a simple fact. Managing that change is a critical and mandatory element of a successful organization. If any organization, public or private, isn't willing to change, that organization will surely fail. Organizations are made up of people. Since we're all obviously people, we know that we are—at best—leery of change. It's just human nature. We are generally leery of change because we are concerned with how the proposed change will affect us personally. Once we see that there is really nothing for us to personally fear, we usually open our minds and begin supporting the proposed change.

For changes that are imposed upon your area of responsibility from the outside, the critical element is communication. Don't just let a memo on the change or a new policy or procedure suffice for your people. Make sure you make the effort to fully understand how this externally imposed change occurred. In other words, who, what, why, where, and how? Once you've studied the change and its impact, take the time to meet with your people, explain what you know, and allow them to ask questions. If necessary, carry any comments, suggestions, or requests back up to your bosses. Taking the time to implement external changes into your department with this personal touch makes it much easier for your people to receive it, accept it, and ultimately successfully implement it. After all, it's your people who make the change successful, not your bosses.

Jack Welch said, "Change before you have to." This is important to remember. Change from within the organization puts you and your people in the driver's seat, as opposed to externally driven change that forces us to change without input. Internal change should absolutely be encouraged in your area of responsibility. The beautiful thing about internal change is that it comes from your people. They are the experts on how to do their jobs and how to be productive. So any suggestions for change from them should not only be taken seriously but also be enthusiastically received.

I believe we should always understand why we do what we do. If we don't, we should ask. I like to say that we should always respectfully question the status quo. If we don't ask for the why, we may as well just accept things for what they are—and if we do that, we may as well just say that we're done improving ourselves and our organizations. Just as parents should do when their children ask them, bosses should take the time to explain the why to their subordinates. If we don't know the answer to why we do what we do, maybe we should evaluate if there is a better, more efficient, more effective, or safer way to accomplish the task. Many great ideas have been realized simply because someone had the courage to respectfully ask why or question the status quo.

I actually instituted a "process for change" in my organization. It basically encouraged ideas for positive change from all of my people, at all levels of the department. It laid out an easy procedure for them to follow from start to finish. It included an initial presentation of the proposed change to the joint management-labor body for initial approval to move forward for research and development, assignment of a chief officer as a liaison for the project, a time line, a status report schedule, input from the organization, final presentation for approval, and steps for implementation. If the initial presentation did not result in approval by the labor-management group to move forward, reasons for denial or a necessary action list prior to resubmitting were issued.

Some very effective change resulted from our process for change. I remember very clearly the day a small group of young captains came to us with a proposal that would essentially make many of the engine-company standard operating guidelines (SOGs) I implemented years before obsolete. Ironically, I found myself in these captains' situation twenty years earlier when I had respectfully challenged the then-status-quo SOGs. Of course, my initial thought while these young captains were justifying their position was that there was nothing wrong with our present engine-company SOGs because I had developed many of them years ago. However, I soon returned to my senses and realized that they had indeed presented adequate justification to allow their ideas to move through the research-and-development stage, and I am so glad I did. While the entire process from justification to implementation took over eighteen months, it resulted in a far more efficient fire-suppression platform for our citizens and a much safer environment for my firefighters.

When you realize that your people are the experts in what they do, and you encourage them to implement positive change from within, you not only improve the efficiency of your department or area of responsibility but also empower your people to use their imagination and self-motivation to improve the organization as a whole, while continuously increasing their level of loyalty to the company.

Whether the change is externally imposed or internally driven, here are some basic steps that should be considered for successful implementation.

1. Communicate the reason for and associated benefits of the change to the organization.

2. Communicate the vision and associated goals for implementation.

3. Take the time to educate those who are resistant to the change and attempt to gain their support.

4. Form an implementation team from a cross section of the organization or from within your area of responsibility.

5. Implement the change.

6. Continue to revisit the change and make any needed adjustments.

7. If the implemented change is ultimately determined to be effective, give credit to your people.

8. If the implemented change is ultimately determined to be ineffective, take responsibility and go back to the drawing board.

Workbook for Managers

Managing Time

Do you manage your time by first determining what you are actually responsible for in your position?

_____

_____

How can I improve?

_____

_____

_____

_____

_____

_____

_____

_____

_____

_____

_____

_____

_____

_____

_____

_____

_____

_____

Do you maximize the use of your electronic calendar?

_____

_____

How can I improve?

_____
_____
_____
_____
_____
_____
_____
_____
_____
_____
_____
_____
_____
_____
_____
_____
_____
_____
_____
_____
_____
_____
_____

Do you manage your time by prioritizing your day and realistically determining what you can accomplish?

_____

_____

How can I improve?

_____

_____

_____

_____

_____

_____

_____

_____

_____

_____

_____

_____

_____

_____

_____

_____

_____

Do you monitor the workloads of your people?

_____

_____

Are you careful not to delegate too much?

_____

_____

Are you careful not to overburden them?

_____

_____

How can I improve?

_____

_____

_____

_____

_____

_____

_____

_____

_____

_____

_____

_____

Managing Programs

Do you manage your programs by establishing missions for each to determine if the program is necessary? What do you do to keep your team focused?

_____

_____

How can I improve?

_____

_____

_____

_____

_____

_____

_____

_____

_____

_____

_____

_____

_____

_____

_____

_____

_____

Have you established associated performance measures to assist you in the ongoing evaluation of whether your program is truly meeting its mission?

_____

_____

How can I improve?

_____

_____

_____

_____

_____

_____

_____

_____

_____

_____

_____

_____

_____

_____

_____

_____

_____

_____

_____

Do you make necessary adjustments to your program as determined by evaluating performance-measure results?

_____

_____

How can I improve?

_____

_____

_____

_____

_____

_____

_____

_____

_____

_____

_____

_____

_____

_____

_____

_____

_____

_____

_____

Managing Special Projects

Do you manage special projects by clearly stating what the special project is to your people?

_____

_____

Do you establish clear and understandable parameters about how much creativity and ingenuity employees will be allowed in completing it?

_____

_____

Do you clearly state what its level of importance is in relation to the employee's normal workload?

_____

_____

How can I improve?

_____

_____

_____

_____

_____

_____

_____

_____

Are you careful not to continually assign special projects to the same top performers, to avoid the risk of burning them out?

_____

_____

How can I improve?

_____

_____

_____

_____

_____

_____

_____

_____

_____

_____

_____

_____

_____

_____

_____

_____

_____

_____

_____

_____

Do you establish the general parameters associated with your special projects for your people, including who is in charge, what the budget is, when status reports are due, and what the deadline is?

_____

_____

How can I improve?

_____

_____

_____

_____

_____

_____

_____

_____

_____

_____

_____

_____

_____

_____

_____

_____

_____

_____

_____

_____

As the manager, do you empower your people to complete the special project by utilizing their creativity and ingenuity, while you monitor progress with an open mind and without micromanaging?

_____

_____

How can I improve?

_____

_____

_____

_____

_____

_____

_____

_____

_____

_____

_____

_____

_____

_____

_____

_____

Managing Budgets

Do you understand the critical aspect of managing budgets?

_____

_____

How can I improve?

_____

_____

_____

_____

_____

_____

_____

_____

_____

_____

_____

_____

_____

_____

_____

_____

_____

_____

_____

Do you have an overall understanding of your organization's budgetary system, including the various funds, principle revenue sources, and major expenditures?

_____

_____

How can I improve?

_____

_____

_____

_____

_____

_____

_____

_____

_____

_____

_____

_____

_____

_____

_____

_____

_____

_____

Do you understand the budgetary process of your organization, including preparing for the upcoming budget year and monitoring the current budget status?

_____

_____

How can I improve?

_____

_____

_____

_____

_____

_____

_____

_____

_____

_____

_____

_____

_____

_____

_____

_____

_____

_____

_____

_____

Do you understand the importance of budgetary standards such as GASB or FASB?

_____

_____

How can I improve?

_____

_____

_____

_____

Do you understand the importance of monitoring revenue versus expenditures on a continual basis?

_____

_____

Do you understand how to make adjustments as necessary?

_____

_____

How can I improve?

_____

_____

_____

_____

_____

_____

Do you include your people in the budgetary process to gain their necessary input and mentor them?

_____

_____

How can I improve?

_____

_____

_____

_____

_____

_____

_____

_____

_____

_____

_____

_____

_____

_____

_____

_____

_____

_____

_____

_____

Do you keep your bosses and subordinates informed of the budgetary status in your area of responsibility?

_____

_____

How can I improve?

_____

_____

_____

_____

_____

_____

_____

_____

_____

_____

_____

_____

_____

_____

_____

_____

_____

_____

Managing Committees

Do you manage committees by first determining that the committee is, in fact, even necessary?

_____

_____

How can I improve?

_____

_____

_____

_____

_____

_____

_____

_____

_____

_____

_____

_____

_____

_____

_____

_____

_____

Do you keep the committees small enough to manage but large enough to benefit from the diversity of the group?

_____

_____

How can I improve?

_____

_____

_____

_____

_____

_____

_____

_____

_____

_____

_____

_____

_____

_____

_____

_____

_____

_____

_____

Do you ensure that the meetings you schedule are actually necessary?

_____

_____

How can I improve?

_____

_____

_____

_____

_____

_____

_____

_____

_____

_____

_____

_____

_____

_____

_____

_____

_____

_____

_____

_____

_____

Do you publish agendas for your committee meetings along with time lines for each item?

_____

_____

How can I improve?

_____

_____

_____

_____

_____

_____

_____

_____

_____

_____

_____

_____

_____

_____

_____

_____

_____

_____

Do you ensure transparency by distributing committee meeting minutes throughout the organization?

_____

_____

How can I improve?

_____

_____

_____

_____

_____

_____

_____

_____

_____

_____

_____

_____

_____

_____

_____

_____

_____

_____

_____

Managing Conflict

Do you embrace constructive conflict as being good for the organization by debating important issues, making good decisions, and moving forward?

_____

_____

How can I improve?

_____

_____

_____

_____

_____

_____

_____

_____

_____

_____

_____

_____

_____

_____

_____

_____

Do you understand that constructive conflict allows us to embrace diversity of opinion and increase the odds of making the right decision?

_____

_____

How can I improve?

_____

_____

_____

_____

_____

_____

_____

_____

_____

_____

_____

_____

_____

_____

_____

_____

_____

_____

_____

Do you understand how constructive conflict generates support and buy-in by the participants?

_____

_____

How can I improve?

_____

_____

_____

_____

_____

_____

_____

_____

_____

_____

_____

_____

_____

_____

_____

_____

_____

_____

_____

_____

Do you understand the importance of establishing clear guidelines for con-structive-conflict sessions to prevent them from becoming deconstructive?

_____

_____

How can I improve?

_____

_____

_____

_____

_____

_____

_____

_____

_____

_____

_____

_____

_____

_____

_____

_____

_____

_____

_____

_____

Managing Change

Do you understand that change must and will occur and that organizations that are unwilling to change will eventually fail?

_____

_____

How can I improve?

_____

_____

_____

_____

_____

_____

_____

_____

_____

_____

_____

_____

_____

_____

_____

_____

_____

_____

Do you understand that the best ideas for change usually come from those who are doing the job?

_____

_____

How can I improve?

_____

_____

_____

_____

_____

_____

_____

_____

_____

_____

_____

_____

_____

_____

_____

_____

_____

_____

_____

_____

Do you use a known template for your people to submit suggested changes as an effective way to encourage internal creativity and positive change?

_____

_____

How can I improve?

_____
_____
_____
_____
_____
_____
_____
_____
_____
_____
_____
_____
_____
_____
_____
_____
_____
_____
_____
_____

When managing change, do you . . .

1. Communicate the reason for the change and its associated benefits to the organization?

   How can I improve?

   _____
   _____
   _____
   _____

2. Communicate the vision and associated goals for implementation?

   How can I improve?

   _____
   _____
   _____
   _____

3. Take the time to **educate** those who are resistant to the change and attempt to gain their support?

   How can I improve?

   _____
   _____
   _____
   _____

4. Form an implementation team from a cross section of the organization or from within your area of responsibility?

   How can I improve?

   _____

   _____

   _____

   _____

   _____

5. Implement the change?

   How can I improve?

   _____

   _____

   _____

   _____

   _____

6. Continue to revisit the change and make any needed adjustments?

   How can I improve?

   _____

   _____

   _____

   _____

   _____

7. If the implemented change is ultimately determined to be effective, do you give credit to your people?

How can I improve?

_____

_____

_____

_____

_____

8. If the implemented change is ultimately determined to be ineffective, do you take responsibility and go back to the drawing board?

How can I improve?

_____

_____

_____

_____

_____

_____

Chapter Three: The Leader

Skills and Abilities of the Leader

A definition of strong leadership I've developed over the years is simply the ability to inspire your people to move above and beyond the status quo and to pursue and achieve the organizational vision for the future. There are hundreds of books out there containing a plethora of leadership theories and philosophies. Some of these books are excellent, and if you desire to become knowledgeable in those varied leadership theories and philosophies, I certainly encourage you to read them. But as I stated in the beginning of this book, my focus is not on theories and philosophies. My whole intent is to offer you the down-to-earth practices that I know for a fact work. I know they work because I had to learn most of them on my own—many times, the hard way.

So who actually needs to be a leader or show leadership characteristics? In my opinion, anyone who is responsible for seeing that employees meet the daily mission and work to attain the vision of the organization must be a leader. This is not to say that people in their personal lives don't need to lead themselves or their families to some degree in order to accomplish their goals. For purposes of this book, though, I want to keep the discussion on leading people in the work environment.

Let me be clear: when I speak of leaders being necessary, I am not speaking exclusively of the big boss of the company or agency. Everyone has a boss, unless you're independently wealthy and don't need to work. Even the big boss of your organization answers to someone. In the public sector, the boss answers to city managers, county executive officers, city councils, boards of supervisors, and ultimately, the citizens. In the private sector, the boss answers to a board of directors or—at minimum—the customer or consumer.

Therefore, anyone reading this book reports to or takes direction from someone. As a result, leaders are needed at all levels of an organization. Later in this chapter, I'll make the point that leaders can't do it all. They need to have the ability to harness the knowledge, skills, abilities, and creativeness of those they oversee to meet the mission and attain the vision of the organization. This means that supervisors and managers at all levels need to be leaders. While the military clearly fully understands this concept, we in the public and private sectors often struggle with it. So whether you're a fire marshal, battalion chief, engine-company captain, watch commander, patrol sergeant, training officer, emergency-dispatch supervisor, school principal, production-line manager, charge nurse, lead grocery clerk, maintenance-crew supervisor, train-crew supervisor, union president, office manager, small business owner, or one of a thousand other positions, you truly need to be a leader.

Unfortunately, most organizations leave the leadership aspect out of their training programs, or they wait until an employee is promoted to a supervisor or manager position and then maybe—and I do mean maybe—they begin an attempt to develop that person into a leader. This is crazy! Leadership knowledge, skills, and abilities take years to learn, practice, and master. As I look back at my career, I truly wish I would have become a student of the subject long before I realized it was necessary for my job. When I did realize that I needed leadership knowledge, skills, and abilities, I had to gain them on my own, and usually through my own mistakes.

Before I go any further, I want to give credit to an organization that is an exception to the rule and does indeed take leadership training and development seriously. Our United States Marine Corps does an excellent job in this area. Over the years I've done some fairly extensive research into their program and have gleaned a significant amount of valuable information that I utilized in my fire department training and development program(s). In my opinion, it is an exemplary public-sector organization that all taxpayers should be proud of.

I've already made clear that I believe supervisory, management, and leadership skills are three entirely different disciplines. Even though they seem to be interchangeable terms when listening to people discuss them, they truly are not. Yes, all of them are very important, and at times they may even overlap, but they are definitely different. You can only be so effective overseeing others if you do not demonstrate effective leadership skills and abilities. In fact, you may supervise and manage your area of responsibility very well, and your people may indeed meet the spirit of the organizational mission on a daily basis, but if you are not supporting, developing, and, most of all, inspiring your people to chase and achieve the vision of the organization, in the long run, you're cheating yourself, your people, and your organization.

Whether in business or government, those of us who have been given the responsibility to oversee employees must inspire those same employees to accomplish the established goals and objectives that lead to successfully achieving the respective visions of our organizations. If we're not doing this, our organizations are just wasting time establishing these visions in the first place. Vince Lombardi, one of the all-time great leaders, clearly understood this when he said, "The achievements of an organization are the results of the combined efforts of each individual."

Leadership Capabilities

Leaders are needed at all levels of an organization, not just at the top. Being a leader is not synonymous with rank or title. In fact, informal leaders without rank or title are indispensable in any organization. They are usually the glue that holds everything together. By the way, these are the individuals who should be sought out and developed to become the formal leaders of the future.

Is every employee capable of being a leader? Yes and no. I believe most people are capable of being leaders. But being capable of being a leader and having the desire to become a leader are two very different things. Organizations can certainly make it mandatory for all of their employees to attend leadership classes. In all actuality, that's not a bad idea. Exposing everyone to what is necessary to become a leader would, at the very least, begin to distinguish those who are interested and have the desire to learn more about the subject from those who simply desire to be followers. Additionally, those who don't desire to be leaders will begin to see the importance placed on the subject by their company. Just to clarify: being a follower is not bad. An organization needs both leaders and hardworking, loyal employees to be successful. Back to the point: an individual must have the desire to become a leader, not just the capability.

Ideally, as I alluded to earlier, I believe that teaching supervisors and managers how to be effective leaders should go hand in hand. When teaching supervisory and management skills, leadership concepts should also be incorporated within the curriculum. I've found that those who are interested in promoting to supervisory and management positions within an organization also want to be good leaders. The problem is that no one has really taken the time to teach them what leadership is. They've heard of leadership and have probably even observed it in some form or another in the organization, but to them it's just an intangible word or concept. To make matters worse, many organizations don't even teach supervisory or managerial skills to their people, much less leadership concepts.

If an organization is truly fortunate enough to have effective leaders, these individuals know what to look for in prospective leadership candidates. These leaders can recognize the raw talent and the desire to serve. This is where the concept of leadership can take hold and grow. Leaders demonstrate the necessary skills and have the ability to lead by example. As more and more employees follow these examples and desire to also become effective leaders, the organizational culture begins to change over time. Despite not being sponsored by the organization, effective leadership begins to become the norm. Yes, even if the organization doesn't actively promote effective leadership, those individuals within the organization who not only have the capability to become leaders but also have the desire to become students of leadership can slowly change the culture of an organization.

How does a capable individual with the desire to become an effective leader educate themselves if their company doesn't promote the concept? There are many ways.

1. Read all you can about the subject. There are hundreds of books available on leadership. However, keep in mind that most are intended to teach the theory of leadership, or the many different styles of leadership.

2. Once you know what you're looking for, begin to learn from both good and bad examples in your workplace. This is the way to develop your own leadership style.

3. Practice, practice, practice! Once you start using good leadership skills and find that they do indeed work for you, you'll start believing in your-self as a leader. Before you know it, you are a leader—and others are learn-ing how to be a leader from you.

Act like a Leader

So you believe you have the ability and the desire to become an effective leader. What other minimum qualifications do you need? Well, anyone can attempt to become a good leader, but without already possessing certain in-dividual traits, you will most assuredly face an uphill battle. Understand that I'm not saying you can't overcome deficiencies in the area of personal traits. I am saying, however, that you're going to have some difficulties in proving to people who have known you for some time that you've seriously changed direction and will be consistently demonstrating these new traits.

In my experience, there are certain personal traits that are very important if you are going to lead people. Was I the perfect demonstration of all these traits? Of course I wasn't. I am human, just as you are. Did I try to demonstrate them consistently? Of course I did. But even when I stumbled, I admitted it to myself, learned from it, and strove not to make that same mistake again.

Integrity

This trait is mentioned so often that it becomes almost an automatic answer by candidates when asked what their most important trait or quality is. Be that as it may, it is arguably the most important trait that a leader can possess and demonstrate. As a leader you must have unquestioned integrity. You must practice honesty and truthfulness in everything you say and do. Your people must be able to absolutely trust you and believe everything you say to them. Don't tell them only what you think they want to hear. All it will take is for you to mislead them or shade the truth one time for you to lose your people's confidence in you. You must also follow up and do what you say you will do. Don't be known as just a starter; also be known as a finisher.

Courage

Certainly, having physical courage is important in careers such as the military, high-rise building construction, law enforcement, firefighting, or crab fishing in Alaska, to name but a few. What I'm referring to here is the courage to do what is right. A leader must absolutely have the courage to do what is right, no matter how difficult or uncomfortable it may be. The list is endless: standing up for what is right, even when it's not popular; admitting that you made a mistake; taking responsibility for a mistake made by your people; showing no tolerance of unacceptable behavior; changing negative employee behavior when necessary; or making a tough, ethical decision. These are just a few examples. I promise you, every decision you make as a leader will draw criticism to some degree. You simply will not be able to please everyone in the organization. Being an effective leader is not easy. I repeat: being an effective leader is not easy. It takes a tremendous amount of courage to be a good leader and to do the right thing.

Decisiveness

I talk about the decision-making process of a leader later in the book. What I'm talking about here is the ability of a leader to make a decision in a timely manner. Your people, your customers, and your organization are waiting for you to make a decision when an issue comes up. Of course, this is assuming that due diligence is given for any necessary research, including—when necessary—requesting and considering the opinions of your people. The point here is that dragging your feet or putting off the decision rarely makes the issue better. You must be decisive and make the call so the organization can move forward.

Dependability/Reliability

Everyone has had to depend on someone else at some point. However, in the work environment, a leader must always be dependable not only to his or her subordinates but also to his or her superiors. The employees must be able to rely on their leader for guidance and support. The superiors must be able to rely on the leader to not only carry out the daily mission of the organization but also to inspire the employees to be loyal to the company and work hard toward achieving the organizational vision.

Initiative

Initiative is a valued trait in any employee, but it is absolutely necessary for a leader at any level within an organization. No supervisor wants to have to tell an employee what to do all day long. Clear expectations should be given at the start of the day or shift, and the employee should be capable of completing the assigned tasks. When those tasks are completed, he or she should have enough initiative to come up with a good idea of what else could be proactively accomplished without being told. Likewise, a leader should constantly be aware of the daily mission and projected vision of an organization and be able to keep himself or herself and the employees within those parameters working toward those goals, while at the same time not being afraid to try new ideas or concepts that may improve processes, production, or safety.

Tact

Everyone has a different personality. A leader, despite his or her personality, must have sufficient tact to effectively interact with subordinates and superiors. Simply displaying courtesy and good manners will help you accomplish more than will being rude. Being polite is not a sign of weakness in a leader. Practicing patience and tolerance is also critical. Remember that you are dealing with different personalities and none of them will be exactly like you. Being a leader means you have to make tough decisions—decisions that won't always be popular or that may result in frustration or even hurt feelings in your people. A leader keeps this in mind, and if he or she can deliver these decisions with tact and caring for those who are affected, it will ease the pain and begin the healing for those who didn't get the result they desired. Tact also earns the leader additional respect for how they handled the process.

Fairness

As a leader, you'll be dealing with both personnel and personal issues. You must understand that there are always at least two sides to every story, and you must fully understand both or all of them before making a decision. Always strive to keep an open mind. Try not to prejudge. When it's time to make your decision, fairness must prevail.

Enthusiasm

Granted, it's not easy for everyone to have enthusiasm for his or her job. The secret is obviously finding the right job that makes it possible for us to willingly get up in the morning and enjoy going to work. Even if that's not possible, as a leader, your enthusiasm will pay great dividends for you if you can find a way to demonstrate and instill enthusiasm in your employees. Whatever the mission, try to find enjoyment in doing the job well. Enthusiasm is infectious and contagious; it will definitely spread to your people and, as a result, translate into improved productivity.

Sacrifice

Being an effective leader will require some sacrifice. A leader must be willing to sacrifice time, effort, and, most of all, credit or glory for the good of her people and the organization. Simply put, an effective leader must be willing to sacrifice a little of herself to develop and inspire her people to move the organization forward. A leader isn't a real leader if she believes it's all about her own glory. On the contrary, it's about the glory and success of her people and her organization.

Loyalty

Showing dedication, faithfulness, and loyalty to your organization, your superiors, and of course your subordinates is a trait that will most assuredly earn you respect from above and below. If you have a disagreement or problem with a person or an element of your organization, deal with them or it in private. Externally, there should never be a hint of anything but loyalty perceived from your actions. (This includes starting or perpetuating rumors or negative talk.) This positive image is absolutely essential in building and maintaining esprit de corps or good morale in any organization.

Consistency

None of these aforementioned traits are worth the paper they're written on without practicing and demonstrating them consistently. Consistency is arguably one of the most important traits that a leader can demonstrate. A supervisor or manager who consistently demonstrates the traits of integrity, courage, decisiveness, dependability, initiative, tact, fairness, enthusiasm, and loyalty is on his or her way to becoming an effective leader.

Leaders Appreciate Their People

Organizations, companies, and agencies are not inanimate objects; they are a gathering of people, put together to accomplish a mission. The problems, issues, costs, headaches, and struggles in an organization are usually derived from the people who populate it. On the other hand, the solutions, productivity, and ultimately the success of the organization also result from those same people. The difference is effective leadership.

I became fire chief of my department in the midst of the Great Recession. Where previously I assisted the fire chief in building our organization, I soon found myself involved in overseeing drastic reductions to my beloved fire department. Without the mutual appreciation of my people, and our willingness to work together to get through those extremely difficult times, I would have failed. I want to be clear on this subject. I don't want you to have to read between the lines. You must understand that your people will make or break you. No matter how good a supervisor or manager you are, if you don't put your people first and understand their importance in the big picture, you will never be truly successful. However, if you do understand and believe in this concept, becoming an effective leader will take care of itself. It begins and ends with your people. Repeat after me: "It begins and ends with my people."

Think about it: can you, as a supervisor or manager, achieve the daily mission or successfully realize the vision of your organization by yourself? Of course not. Leading, caring for, developing, supporting, and inspiring your people is the only way to ensure that the mission and the vision of your organization are met—period. Paul O'Neil, former CEO of Alcoa, said, "People have discretionary energy, they won't give it to you if they aren't treated with dignity and respect."

It's not about you. It's about your people and what they can do for your organization. If you are an effective leader to them, the sky is the limit. Understand that I'm not saying you should let your people do whatever they want just to keep them happy. On the contrary, you still have an obligation to supervise them and keep them within the parameters of the guiding documents of the organization. If you're effectively leading them at the same time, those instances of negative behavior will be few and far between.

As leaders, we must also understand the critical importance and relationship between saying the right thing to our people and backing it up with action. In reality, it is quite easy to say the right thing, but the difficulty comes in making sure we support those words with the appropriate actions. There are two ways this can really damage our reputations as leaders. The first is by not completing something we said we would complete—possibly a project or a change of policy. While no one will be able to realistically complete everything he or she starts, when it becomes a predictable process in the eyes of your people, it won't take long before you're known as a big talker, not the type of a leader who gets things done. The other way you can damage your reputation is by expecting your people to act in a certain way but not living up to that expectation yourself. "Do as I say, not as I do" is the lazy leader's mantra. Simply put, you also end up looking like a hypocrite. No one has respect for these kinds of leaders. In fact, can we even call them leaders? (I'm sure as each of you reads this, you can easily remember former or present bosses who exemplify what we're talking about.) Once you reach either one of these points in your career, your effectiveness as a leader is done. Even if you realize you've somehow gotten to this point, overcoming these perceptions will take years. As a result, your subordinates suffer, the team suffers, and, ultimately, the organization suffers. Remember, leaders must walk the talk.

I gave my people whatever I possibly could to help them do their job more safely and efficiently. Firefighting can be very stressful and dangerous work, both physically and emotionally. I would tell them after briefings or addresses that I loved them and to be careful. I would also frequently remind them how fortunate they were to have jobs they enjoyed and to remember to have fun when possible. Yes, it's actually OK to have fun at work. We all have a job to do, but no one says we can't enjoy ourselves while working. Happy employees who know their leaders appreciate and care about them will also be productive employees.

Leaders Appreciate Their Organization's History

An important question for a leader to ask is, "Where did this organization come from?" Truly, how can I help establish, pursue, and eventually achieve an organizational vision for the future if I don't know where the organization came from? How can you expect your people to appreciate the need to chase a vision if they don't know the organizational history? A leader must learn the history of the company. A leader must appreciate the struggles the company has gone through to get to where it is today. A leader must establish a vision, taking into account where the organization has been. Arguably most importantly, a leader must teach his or her people to appreciate that history.

For years I wanted to establish a written history of my fire department. It wasn't until very late in my tenure and through the efforts of some self-motivated individuals that I was able to get this accomplished. The timeliness of this was advantageous as we were in the midst of merging with the other agencies. The result was an established written record of the organization that was issued to each new employee that entered the fire academy. My hope was that this document would become the foundation to their knowledge of where the department came from, and, most importantly, engender an appreciation of those who spilled their blood, sweat, and tears—many times literally—in an effort to improve the organization to the level it is at today. Occasionally when I felt the need to remind an individual to appreciate our department history and the efforts of those who went before him, I would ask if he actually believed this place was created the day before he was hired, just for him. This usually got the point across.

It is extremely important that a leader make the effort to not only learn the history but to appreciate it, and to ensure that it is passed from generation to generation, with the goal of building upon this foundation in the pursuit of a vision of excellence.

The Four *C*s of Leadership

Over the years, I've learned through experience that in order to become a truly effective leader, there are four abilities that one must be able to master, and they all happen to begin with the letter *C*. I call them the four *C*s of Leadership.

Commitment

A leader absolutely must be committed to the organization. Logically, this means the leader is committed to the guiding documents, the core values, the mission, and the vision of the organization. When making decisions, the good of the organization must always be foremost in the leader's mind. Referring to the guiding documents, mission, core values, and vision becomes routine. When this is done, decision making is made much easier.

A committed leader must always be aware of what he or she is saying and who is hearing it. A committed leader does not speak negatively about the organization or its people and, in turn, expects the same from his or her people. Be the example, not the hypocrite.

It is important to remember that being committed to the organization also means the leader must be committed to the employees for whom he or she is responsible. After all, the employees make up the organization, and success is clearly impossible without them. If the leader can inspire his or her people to also maintain a commitment to the organization over a commitment to their own personal desires, organizational success is a no-brainer. And when the organization succeeds, everyone in the organization wins.

Communication

Good leaders listen to their people. They do so because they know that leaders don't have to know everything. They also know that some of the best ideas come from the people who are doing the work. It's only logical. Allow your people to question you, your decisions, and the way things are done (respectfully, of course). The goal is for the organization to be successful, right? Drop your ego and listen to your people. They know you're the boss and have the final say, so you don't need to prove it. Listening to your people is not a sign of weakness. In fact, it will be looked on as a strength through your people's eyes. Let them—no, encourage them to—question everything. They just may have a better way of doing things, so what's the harm in trying something new? If it doesn't work, you can always go back and do it the way you did it before. What have you lost? Nothing. In fact, you've gained reinforcement that you truly were doing things the best way possible. If the new way is better, you've gained efficiency, improved productivity, increased safety for your people, or simply found a better way to do things. By the way, allowing and encouraging your people to question you also forces you to know your stuff before you present it to them, and this makes you a more informed and competent leader.

How important is it for a leader to be able to communicate with his or her people? How is anything going to get done within your organization if you don't? Communication is critical for a leader. When I say communicate with your people, I mean in both directions. Information flow must go down to the newest, lowest-seniority employee you are responsible for. It must also go the other way. Your employees must also be able to pass their thoughts, ideas, feelings, and questions back up to you and your bosses.

It is just as critical to make sure that your bosses are aware of what is going on under your watch. What is the condition of your area of responsibility? How are your people? What projects are you working on? What are their present statuses? Is there anything that they should be aware of? Do they know what may be coming their way? Remember, your bosses don't want to be surprised with an issue popping up in front of them any more than you do. I had to learn this the hard way as a new division chief. I thought, purely out of ignorance, that I shouldn't bother my boss with what was routinely going on within my scope of authority unless it was significant. I figured if he trusted me enough to oversee the division, he didn't need regular briefings from me. What I didn't grasp at the time was that, while he delegated his authority to me, he couldn't delegate his responsibility to me. He, as the fire chief, was ultimately responsible for everything I or my people did or didn't do. Basically, he was caught off guard with a compliment (I was thankful that it wasn't a complaint) paid to him by the city manager about an exceptional rescue my people had performed the previous day. As a result, the boss made it very clear to me, and rightfully so, that he not only required regular status reports but also required immediate notification on anything that he may be questioned on (something I quickly learned the value of when I was promoted to his position).

An effective leader must continually communicate the contents of the strategic or business plan of the organization to his or her people. This includes the daily mission, the vision, and the core values. While these documents should be accessible to all of your people to reference at will, they must on a regular basis hear it from their leader. There must never be any doubt in their minds what is expected of them or where they are going. This is crucial, no matter what level of a supervisor or manager you are.

An effective leader must continually evaluate his or her teams and communicate to them how they are doing. Are they meeting organizational performance measures? As a result, are they meeting the daily mission of the organization? If not, it's up to the leader to help them adjust their direction and get back on track. Are they working toward the vision of the organization? Are they headed in the right direction? They want to know that they are contributing to the organization.

An effective leader keeps his or her people informed on what is going on in the organization. There may be memos or emails issued from the top, informing everyone of new policies, procedures, or guidelines, but that in itself is not enough. Are you verbally interpreting this new information for them? Are you answering their questions? If you can't, are you finding the answers for them?

Your people need and deserve to hear all information that may pertain to or affect them. This includes good news, bad news, and anything in between. Except for rare bits of information that must remain confidential, such as personnel issues or contract negotiations, all information in regard to the organization should be shared with them.

To your people, you are the voice of the organization. They must be able to count on you to keep them informed. They must also be able to count on you to carry their questions, opinions, ideas, and concerns to the top. I wanted, needed, and fully expected my subordinate leaders to bring that information to me. I wanted and needed to know what was on the minds of my hardworking people who, by the way, were making the organization (and me) look good.

Collaborate

Collaborating can simply be described as working together to accomplish a goal, solve a problem, or overcome an obstacle. Supervisors, managers, and even leaders sometimes think they can (or are expected to) accomplish, solve, or overcome problems or issues by themselves due to their position in the organization. This will lead to three things:

1. lack of original or outside-the-box ideas and solutions due to lack of diversity of opinion;

2. poor time management;

3. decreased odds of coming up with a good result.

Working together or collaborating can and will allow you to take full advantage of the diversity of opinions, skill sets, and original ideas from your people, saving time through the process and increasing the odds of coming up with a good result in the end.

A by-product of collaborating is strengthening the relationship between different groups or teams within the organization. Trust and confidence between individuals and groups of individuals will emerge and develop as a result of working together to accomplish a goal, solve a problem, or overcome an obstacle. One of the most common examples of this is when management and labor work collaboratively. As long as both groups keep in mind that the success of the overall organization must prevail and that the commitment to that organization must be maintained above and beyond the individuals and separate groups, incredible results are possible from this collaboration. This was clearly the case in our fire department during the Great Recession. Without the collaboration between management and labor, the organization would have been devastated by budget reductions, drastically reducing the service to the community. I would venture to say that as fire chief, maybe 10 percent of the eventual answers to the budget problems came from me, and the rest came from labor. The only thing I can really take credit for during those difficult times was understanding that I wasn't the smartest person in the room. However, I was smart enough to know that my people were a giant think tank of ideas and I only had to ask for their help. As Earl Nightingale is credited with saying, "None of us is as smart as all of us."

Compromise

We're human; no one likes to compromise. This is simply a fact of life, both personally and professionally. But what actually happens when leaders aren't willing to compromise in our organizations? Nothing. That's what happens: nothing. In other words, the organization will not move forward; it simply becomes content with the status quo, and in doing so begins to slip into mediocrity and eventual failure.

Compromising is important whether the leader is dealing with the boss, subordinates, peers, or organized labor. Think about it: isn't it better to compromise and get 50 percent of what you want than to not compromise and get 0 percent of what you want? More importantly, isn't it better to continue to move the organization forward in small, continuous steps of progress by compromising than to stubbornly allow the organization to become stagnate and unproductive?

An important prerequisite that must be established in the working environment prior to effective compromise taking place is trust. Without trust, neither party will be willing to compromise. For example, during contract negotiations, both sides have to trust that the other is bargaining in good faith. Without trust there will be no ability to compromise, and without the ability to compromise, we know what follows: nothing. The point is, leaders must first create an environment based upon trust to generally accomplish anything, and more specifically to earn the ability to utilize the tool of compromise, so the organization can move forward.

Compromising is not a sign of weakness in a leader. Compromising with your team members says to them that you value their input and positions on issues that affect the organization. Being a leader does not mean that you have to always be right or get your way. The ability to compromise on organizational issues and move forward is a sign of strength in a leader.

Of course, there may be certain issues or positions that a leader will be unwilling or unable to compromise on. However, these situations should be few and far between. Remember, if you are truly committed to the organization, you will want to put its interests above your interests in order to move it forward and, as a result, make it successful. The willingness to compromise when necessary is a critical aspect of leading your organization to success.

Leaders Train Their People

As an engine-company captain, I wanted to make sure my company was the best trained in the fire department. I wanted to be prepared for whatever emergency we were dispatched to next. My philosophy was that the citizens were paying for a professional service and expected us to perform swiftly, efficiently, and effectively when they called 911 on the worst days of their lives. I had an obligation to meet that expectation. We trained or drilled every shift for two hours, and we actually enjoyed it. We were constantly coming up with new things to train on. The better we got, the better we wanted to be. We continually improved as a team and were rewarded every time we came back from an emergency knowing that we met the expectations of our citizens. I retained this philosophy throughout my career as a captain, battalion chief, training officer, and operations division chief. I believed this so intently that, as fire chief, I set our top two organizational priorities as follows:

1. We will remain operationally ready to respond to emergencies.

2. We will train to be the best we can be for those same emergencies.

How in the world can you ever expect your people to accomplish anything if you don't train them? Hopefully your organization understands this point and has an effective training program with its own mission and vision statements in place, based on and referenced to mandates, standards of the industry, and best practices. Ideally, these programs will feature a database that includes all of the required and preferred training for each individual, a system that is documented (accurate training records are critical) and available for every employee in the organization to access, and goals that are accepted and supported by the leadership of the organization. You should develop a program that trains new employees in the basics of their jobs (including those personal skills that help make employees more efficient and effective in their jobs and prepare individuals for the next step up the promotional ladder, including supervisory, management, and leadership skills). You should also offer continuing education in all of these areas. Consider this quote from an unknown source: "When you maximize the potential of your individuals—you maximize the potential of your team."

Pay attention to your people's job performance or their performance on promotional examinations. If they're not performing to your or the organization's expectations, you need to look at yourself and the organization before you criticize your employees. Ask yourself, "Have we really given them the training they need to perform at a level that makes them and the organization successful?"

There was a huge training void in my organization, and it became very apparent to me early on in my career. As I rose through the ranks, I worked with others who had the passion for spending a great deal of time to develop a complete training program for the department, including those areas I mentioned above. This took a tremendous amount of effort, but it was worth it. While I was never totally satisfied with the program and never felt like it was complete, I look back and see that we had one of the best-trained fire departments in the country. Even though budget reductions reduced the department to a fraction of its earlier size, I would have compared them to any fire department in the nation as to the product they produced while meeting our daily mission of service to the community.

However, not many organizations have training programs this thorough. If that is the case in your organization, as a leader, you need to step up and fill the void. It is your responsibility (whatever your actual position or rank; if you oversee people—you're responsible) to see that your people are adequately trained for the present and the future. If you don't, your people and your organization will not be productive and may even fail.

There are many ways to see that your people are getting the training they need. Find out what skills or information they need or want and see what is available. It could be as simple as assigning self-study, bringing an expert in from the outside, or recruiting the talents of someone within your organization who is a subject-matter expert. It could be as simple as holding discussion or brainstorming sessions on a subject.

If you are uncomfortable getting in front of your people and spear-heading training sessions, you need to get comfortable. There is no better way to get comfortable than by actually doing it. You may not be as smooth as you wish you could be at first, but your people will overlook that. They will be grateful that you care enough to make the effort. You'll also build their trust and confidence in you as a leader.

It's equally important for you as a leader to actually involve yourself in the training. This shows your people that you wouldn't ask them to do any-thing you wouldn't do yourself. It also shows that you are constantly trying to maintain and even improve your skills and that you are not above getting in the trenches with them. Most importantly, it helps you to stay current on what you're asking your people to do on a daily basis.

I attempted to be present at as many training sessions as possible in my organization. I made sure the schedule didn't overwhelm me to the point that I didn't have time to train with my people. By the way, it is very easy to use your full calendar as an excuse not to be out training with your employ-ees. You must make it a point not to let this happen. (Remember what I talked about in regards to time management?) If you do allow your schedule to prevent you from participating in training with your people, you will lose that connection with the very individuals who are making you look good every day—and that can be catastrophic to your ability to lead.

A Leader's Decision-Making Process

I love this quote by Albert Camus: "Life is the sum of all your choices." Great words to ponder, aren't they? I taught my kids that every decision they make affects the rest of their lives. My point in teaching them this was to force them to slow down and think about the consequences of the decisions they make in their lives. I also taught them that if they find that they made the wrong decision, it's OK to admit they made a mistake and to change direction. I taught them about decision making because of what I had learned in life and in my career.

There is a decision-making model that has served me well over the years. As both my life and professional experiences increased, it became necessary to further develop this model. As a division chief, and continuing as the fire chief, I posted a copy of this decision-making model on the wall across from my desk for easy reference. I found it to be very useful for both ordinary and significant problems, issues, dilemmas, or situations:

1. The Discovery Phase includes gathering all associated facts and understanding the whole problem. Do your research.

2. The Consulting Phase includes consulting with peers, seniors, and yes, at times, even subordinates. (Especially if your final decision will affect them. Why wouldn't you? They're the ones who have to live with your

decision, and they're the ones who actually decide whether or not they want to make it work). A confident leader isn't threatened by asking subordinates for their opinions, and she welcomes wild-card or out-of-the box options. Remember, the more diverse your team is, the more out-of-the box their suggestions may be—and many times, this is exactly what a leader needs to hear.

3. The Options Phase includes listing all viable options, then asking the following ethical questions about each option:

A. Is it legal? Will I be breaking a guiding document or law?

B. Is it fair and balanced to all concerned?

C. Is it in accordance with our core values and mission?

D. How will I feel about myself when I look in the mirror tomorrow? (Ethics)

4. The Action Phase includes making your decision and carrying it out.

5. The Monitoring Phase includes monitoring and evaluating the results of the decision and making adjustments as needed, including admitting that you made a mistake and need to go back to step 1.

The vast majority of your decisions will allow you to take the time to work through all of the above steps. This will greatly increase your chances of making the right decisions. Additionally, it allows for people to be human and make mistakes. When we discover that we could have made a better decision, we should not be afraid to admit it and change course with the right decision. In the long run, we gain more respect for admitting our mistakes than for trying to stand by poor decisions.

Again, this model has served me well over the years. I followed it closely, and I highly recommend that leaders at every level of an organization utilize something similar.

Whether you use my decision-making model, someone else's, or one you've developed from your own experiences, it really doesn't matter. The point is that when leaders face dilemmas, a decision eventually has to be made, and using a filter or model is a big help. Putting off making a decision doesn't help the situation; it usually complicates it or makes it worse. I promise you that you will never please everyone involved. So if you're waiting for that perfect decision that everyone will support to drop on your desk, you're wasting your and everyone else's time. Use a decision-making model, and then make the damn decision. If it turns out not to be the right one, you can always go back and start over. Don't be afraid to make the call.

Train your people to use decision-making models, and then trust them to make as many decisions as possible. You should not have to make all the decisions in your area of responsibility. If you have good people and if you've trained them well, decentralize as much decision making as you can. Let your people grow and learn. Mistakes will be made, but in the long run, trust in and develop the decision-making skills of your people. When this investment is made, it will benefit your employees and your company, and you will also earn the benefits of enhanced loyalty and respect from your team.

When I was first promoted to the rank of battalion chief, I found myself responsible for the actions of six or seven very seasoned fire captains. Several of these individuals were Vietnam veterans as well as aggressive, salty firefighters I had looked up to for years. So you can imagine my surprise when, on our first shift working together, each one of them called me up and laid out his day for me, seeking my approval. While I was perplexed at why this was occurring, for the first two shifts, I gave them my OK to proceed. On the third shift, however, I began to ask them why they felt the need to gain permission from me to schedule their day. Their answers shocked me. They basically told me that this was the way it had always been done on this particular shift and that it was expected of them by their previous battalion chiefs.

So here I had mature, experienced, trained individuals, capable of making life-and-death decisions 24/7 on the emergency scene, who were actually expected to ask their boss to approve their schedule of activities for the day. Can you say ridiculous?

The following shift, I met with each of those captains and explained that unless they had a problem for which they specifically needed my help, they did not to seek my approval to schedule their days. I told them I trusted them to make their own mission-based, core-value-oriented decisions. I also told them that they if I needed to coach them from time to time to help improve their decision-making abilities, I would do so. Otherwise, I wanted them to develop their own decision-making matrix or filter based upon the guiding documents of the department—and then utilize it. While it took a couple of them a little time to transition to where I wanted them to be, in the end, they all received my praise for becoming great mission-based, core-value-oriented decision makers.

While most decisions we make are not emergency in nature, I would like to briefly touch on those decisions that don't allow us sufficient time to use a model or filter as discussed above. Emergency decisions are made every day by those in the emergency services and the military. The very nature of these industries places the leaders and their people in dangerous situations. While the job must be completed, the decisions made have very real implications on the physical well-being of their people.

Having to learn on my own through the school of hard knocks, I never became the leader I truly desired to be. However, I did realize early on that having the responsibility of leading others was a privilege. I was often in awe of the talents, abilities, drive, and passion of my people and what they would accomplish. I loved them and told them so. At the same time, I had the responsibility to lead them into potentially harmful situations in order to save lives and property—the core mission of the fire service. Balancing the mission of your organization with the safety of your people is the dilemma those of us with the "burden of command" assume.

These decisions are necessarily made within seconds and based basically on two things: training and experience. While employees will gain experience over time, supervisors, managers, and leaders must ensure that their people receive the required training to make emergency decisions and that the training is as realistic as possible. This is especially critical for new employees. Seasoned employees have years of emergency experience to help them make split-second decisions, but new employees have very little history to call upon, so they must rely solely upon their training.

Closely related and also critical in emergency decision-making situations is intuition, also known as that "little voice." While we can't rely upon intuition to be correct 100 percent of the time, we certainly do need to consider it. As I see it, your intuition is based on the totality of your life experiences. Obviously, the most dependable intuition will reside in the most realistically trained and experienced employee. But even a newer but well-trained employee begins developing an intuition that must be at least consulted when making an emergency decision.

On a morning in July 2002, I was working at my desk when the sky outside my window grew dark with black smoke. The sounds of small explosions rattled my office. When I went outside to take a look, I saw a huge black column of smoke rising from a roofing-company yard a quarter mile away. After calling the report in to dispatch, I donned my gear and drove toward the incident. As I was driving down the street, I was met by fifteen to twenty employees running from the yard, yelling that the large pressurized tank truck was going to explode. As I pulled over adjacent to the yard to get an initial look at the situation, I observed what the employees were referring to. What appeared to be a liquified tar or asphalt substance was on fire and flowing through the yard. In its path were propane containers of various sizes. Some had already exploded, while others were venting from their relief valves. At the center of the yard was a bobtail-style truck with a tank containing six hundred gallons of propane. It was surrounded by fire, and its relief valve was venting like a flamethrower. I took a deep breath.

This wasn't going to be just another day at the office, I realized.

This incident was actually just outside my city limits in a neighboring volunteer fire district. The one chief officer who was on the scene from that fire district quickly gave me operational command of the incident. After sizing up the situation and determining the facts, probabilities, and possibilities, it was decision-making time—*emergency* decision-making time. My training told me this was a very dangerous situation with the possibility of a quarter-mile-diameter boiling-liquid/expanding-vapor explosion. Our training tells us that this is a "loser" situation in which everyone—including the fire department—should immediately vacate the area. Sadly, there are tragic examples to look back at in history that justify this philosophy. However, there was a problem: it was going to take up to twenty minutes to evacuate everyone in the immediate area, including a very large, two-story office complex (which was inside my city limits) adjacent to the yard. So while my training said to run, my intuition—my little voice—told me to stay and hold this time bomb at bay in order to give the police department time to evacuate the area. I allowed my intuition to override my training. There was no way I could warrant running before I knew everyone was out of the blast area.

Within a few minutes, I had two alarms of fire resources arriving that I quickly put to work trying to cool the exposed tank, in the hopes of preventing an explosion, as well as cooling the many smaller tanks in the area. In the end, the efforts paid off. The large tank never exploded, an outcome that seemed unbelievable, given the severe damage it received.

I still proudly remember the professionalism and composure that both fire and law enforcement personnel demonstrated that day in the face of what could have very easily been collectively our last days on the job. Subsequent analysis and critiques produced varied opinions on whether we should have stayed and attacked or immediately left the area; however, I never regretted my decision. I am glad I was able to evaluate the situation quickly based on my training and intuition, trust myself, and make the call to put my people in harm's way for the right reasons, resulting in a positive outcome.

In my opinion, the most important aspect of making significant decisions—emergency or nonemergency in nature—is trusting yourself. Trust yourself when you suspect this really is the significant issue, dilemma, or situation you think it is, and it's happening now or about to happen. Trust yourself when you think you need to run this through your decision-making filter or access your training and experience, and always listen to that "little voice." Trust yourself when you have to make a decision that won't be popular. Trust yourself when you make the decision. And when the situation changes, more information becomes available, or for any reason you believe you need to adjust your previous decision, trust yourself and adjust it.

Leaders Understand the Power of Yes and No

They are two seemingly simple words: yes and no. Two simple words with so much meaning and so much power. Leaders must understand this. As discussed previously, a leader who utilizes an effective decision-making filter will greatly increase the odds of making good decisions in relation to significant organizational dilemmas or quandaries. However, practically speaking, every decision a leader must make won't necessarily require the time for thorough research. Some questions simply require a thoughtful yes-or-no answer.

Early in my career, when trying to effect positive change with a new way of doing things, I often heard, "No, that's not the way we do things around here," or "No, we've always done it this way." (Heaven forbid they would want to take a chance and let a young, motivated employee try a new way of getting the job done.) Instead, they found it easier to just say no. I remember being so frustrated when I'd get that answer. I was willing to do all the research and related work and to take all the responsibility for any failure. Even so, I rarely even got the chance to fully explain what I was proposing, much less a chance to make the idea succeed. Is this any way to develop and inspire an employee? Fortunately, as employees like myself began to be promoted through the ranks of the department, we were slowly able to change this attitude and move it to a point where everyone's ideas were considered as potential positive change. Think about it: if no supervisor, manager, or leader in your company ever took a chance on their people and said, "Yes, I will support you and give you an opportunity to succeed," what kind of an organization would you be working for? (Or, sadly, maybe you do work in that organization.) Instead of saying, "No, we can't do that because of these obstacles," leaders should consider saying, "Yes, let's move forward, try to overcome these obstacles, and make this viable idea or concept work to better our organization." Not only does the employee benefit by growing, developing, and gaining confidence, but also the organization improves with increased efficiency and productivity through the implementation of these fresh new ideas, contributed by its own inspired people.

Now, don't misunderstand me: there are times when the leader's answer should be no. If a request is not in line with guiding documents, mission statement, or core values, or not foreseen to be in the overall best interest of the organization, the answer should be no. The leader has an obligation to protect the organization and its people. However, when saying no to his or her subordinates, the leader should always take the time to explain why the answer is no. When a leader simply says, "No, because I said so," or "No, because I'm the boss," without explanation or a plan of improvement for the next time the item is presented, no one benefits. If it's not good for the employees' morale or development, it's also not good for the leader's reputation.

The leader must also remember that she has an obligation to protect herself and her subordinates. A good leader understands that she must muster the courage to tell her boss no. "No, I can't take on anymore projects," or "No, my people shouldn't have to do this," or "No, I don't think this is a good idea," or "No, I don't believe this is in line with our guiding documents." Again, these are only examples, and of course whenever one takes an opposing view with one's boss, it must be done with respect and tact, and obviously for a good reason. The point is that there will be a time when a leader—to protect himself and his subordinates—will need to make a stand. Of course, this is not an easy thing to do, and each leader must decide at what point it is necessary. In the end, you may be ordered to carry out the directive anyway. However, if and when this type of situation occurs, the leader will generally gain respect from his subordinates for standing up for them. If the boss is truly a leader, he or she will appreciate the subordinate leader having the courage to stand up for what he or she believes is right.

During the Great Recession, I remember very well standing before the city manager in passionate disagreement with how my people were being perceived and treated by the city leadership. These were extremely difficult times, and all parties were under a tremendous amount of stress. However, because we were dealing with the potential of my people actually losing their jobs, there was no question—I had to protect them. To his credit, the city manager not only allowed me to voice my position (rather strongly, at times) but also considered my suggestions. In the end, while my department budget was slashed and a significant amount of positions were eliminated, we were able to negotiate and compromise on how the people in these positions would vacate them. Bottom line, no one was laid off on the spot, for which I was grateful.

Leaders Know They Can't Do It All

No matter how good you think you are or how much you think you can accomplish, you need to realize that you are only human. You simply cannot do it all. Leaders must learn to delegate. There are four huge benefits to delegating:

First, as an organization you will all accomplish more.

Second, as a leader, you are freed up to focus on the bigger-picture issues for which you are responsible.

Third, you utilize the expertise of your people.

Fourth, you indirectly mentor and develop those same people by asking them to utilize their problem-solving abilities, ingenuity, and creativity.

Before you can delegate effectively, you need to fully understand the definitions and meanings of a couple of key words: responsibility and authority.

My favorite one-word definition for responsibility is "answerable." If you are responsible for something or someone, you are also answerable for them as well as their success or failure.

My favorite one-word definition for authority is "power." Simply put, when you delegate a task to someone, you give them the authority, or power, to carry out that task. However, you are still responsible or answerable for the outcome. In other words, a leader can delegate authority, but he or she cannot delegate responsibility.

So once a leader understands the difference between responsibility and authority, he or she simply has to be thorough with the instructions and parameters of the delegation to the subordinate, monitor the progress, offer support as needed without micromanaging, keep an open mind, and empower his or her people to be innovative and creative. In the end, a leader gives credit to those people for the positive result and takes personal responsibility for a negative result. Ronald Reagan said it well: "Surround yourself with the best people you can find, delegate authority, and don't interfere as long as the policy you've decided upon is being carried out."

Leaders Act as Professionals

Professional is a word that is sometimes hard to define, but we all recognize it when we see it. And isn't that the point when you're a leader? Those around you, including your peers, subordinates, and superiors, should clearly be able to recognize you as a professional. One common interpretation of the word professional is a person with specific training and education that qualifies that person to be associated with his or her particular profession. Another common connotation describes a mindset of maintaining and projecting a positive, businesslike manner in the work environment, thereby instilling confidence in others.

What are some of the traits that set you apart as a professional? The ones that are important to me are appearance, communication skills, competence, education, self-awareness, and deportment.

Appearance

One's appearance is generally what gives us the first perception of a person's level of professionalism. Does he have good personal hygiene? Is she well groomed? Are his clothes or uniform clean and pressed? Do her clothes or uniform fit properly? Are his shoes shined? A good impression usually starts with that initial perception about one's appearance, and, of course, you only get one chance to make a first impression.

That being said, you can't always judge a book by its cover. Appearance certainly isn't the only criteria for which one should be judged as professional or not. However, one's initial appearance goes a long way in portraying the professional image that a leader should want to portray.

Communication Skills

The need to improve personal communication skills is often overlooked by leaders. A leader's ability to lead her people to achieve a vision or to simply get things done is directly related to her ability to communicate that vision to the very people that need to understand and buy into it.

Understand that I'm not saying a leader has to have a degree in communications to be professional. I'm simply saying that a professional leader is aware of her communication limitations and continually strives to improve and overcome them. Some important areas a leader should consistently be improving in are as follows:

Informal Speech: We should be capable of forming clear thoughts in our minds and relaying those thoughts into clear and complete messages to those we are speaking to, without delivering partial or confusing messages. Just because my thoughts are clear in my head, and I know what I want to say, doesn't mean that I can expect others to read my mind. Am I giving them sufficient background to comprehend? Am I giving them the information in a logical sequence? Am I being clear about what I want them to do with this information? Basically, I must be able to wire my brain and mouth together and actually communicate. If others don't completely understand my message, communication hasn't taken place. Consider this quote from an unknown source: "When you speak, be sure the things you say are an improvement over silence."

Listening: Good listening skills are incredibly important. Complete communication is impossible if the receiver of a verbal message doesn't listen effectively. How frustrating is it when someone we're speaking to isn't really listening to us? The person is either distracted by something else or isn't really interested in what we have to say. Either way, we don't like it. We shouldn't be hypocritical and do it to others. News flash: you don't know everything. Being the boss doesn't automatically make you all knowing. If you seriously try to improve your active listening skill and listen to learn, you may actually retain something valuable. A leader absolutely must request input, truly listen to it, and actually consider it when trying to resolve issues. Without good listening skills, this is simply impossible and will inevitably result in poor decisions being made. This applies to both nonemergency and emergency environments. I've been working on this communication skill for years and probably always will be.

Formal Speech: We've all heard that public speaking is one of the greatest fears for most people. Whether this is true or not, there's no doubt that speaking in front of large groups doesn't come natural to most of us. There's also no doubt that professional leaders must not only have the ability to speak in front of groups of people but also effectively communicate with those groups. How else can a leader directly relate the vision and associated goals of the organization and then inspire those individuals and groups to move forward and actually achieve those goals—and ultimately the vision?

So how does a leader overcome this fear and improve as a public speaker? The answers are really pretty simple. Here are some of my suggestions:

1. Know your material. Why would you speak to a group without being comfortable with the subject matter?

2. Understand that there should be an introduction, a body, and a conclusion to whatever formal speech one gives.

3. Increase the font size and spacing on your script or cheat sheet and use bold print. These tricks will help keep your place.

4. Be aware of your audience; maintain good eye contact with them. Glance down at your document from time to time to stay on track, but make sure you get back to speaking to your audience.

5. Practice, practice, practice. Get out there and do it. With practice comes confidence, and with confidence comes competence. It really is that simple. I took every opportunity to put myself in front of groups of people for just that reason: to improve as a public speaker.

6. Ask for honest feedback from someone you trust after each presentation. Don't just ask for it—listen to it and attempt to improve on it.

Did I ever master public speaking? Of course not. But with each opportunity to practice, my confidence as well as my effectiveness as a communicator improved.

Written Word: Let's be clear: in-person, face to face communication is always more effective when communicating with your people. It's certainly more effective than relying solely on the written word. However, it isn't always possible to have face-to-face communication, and usually any significant face-to-face exchange of information should be followed up with some form of written summary or confirmation. However, writing skills are no different than other forms of communication; unless you constantly strive to improve, you won't reach your potential as a professional leader who has the ability to effectively communicate with your people. How do I get better?

1. As in formal speaking, your writing should also include an introduction, body, and conclusion.

2. Always proofread your draft document. If it's a formal document, have several other people proofread it. The key here is other people; don't edit your own work.

3. Practice, practice, practice! It won't take long before you begin to see improvement in your writing.

Additional thoughts on communication:

1. Consider which form of communication will be the most effective for each situation.

2. Remember that face-to-face is usually the most effective method of communication. The receiver can observe facial expressions and other body language to help comprehend the message, and the sender can more easily determine if the message is fully and correctly understood.

3. As the sender of a message, don't assume the receiver of the message knows the history or background of what you're referencing. Be complete with the information you're sending.

4. If you, as the receiver of a message, are unsure of the meaning or intent, ask for clarification. "Miscommunication" is not "communication."

5. Follow up important verbal communication with a written confirmation. We're all human and prone to forgetting (or at least not remembering) the original message, so put it in writing.

6. Use texting for its intended use: the transmission of short messages. Do not use it as a replacement or other more effective methods. It is very easy to misunderstand texts. I'm embarrassed to tell you that I once argued with my second-in-command for over twenty minutes via texting. When I finally came out of my trance and thought to actually call him on the phone, we resolved our argument in thirty seconds. In fact, there never should have been an argument in the first place; we both totally misunderstood each other through the act of texting. I learned a very important lesson that day.

7. Take a breath and reevaluate the decision to send an emotional email or text message. Once you hit send, you have no control over how it will be interpreted or what will be its final destination. Yep, another lesson I learned the hard way.

8. In the end, the best evaluation of your communication skills as a leader is determined by the actions of your subordinates.

Competence

How important is it to us that our leaders are technically competent in the job they are asking us to do? Is it important at all? To me—and I believe to most —it is very important. In fact, in reference to the purpose of this book, I would go even further and say that it's more important, even critical, that bosses be competent as supervisors, managers, and leaders, in addition to being competent in those tasks they're asking their subordinates to be competent in on a daily basis. Organizations are usually pretty good at ensuring their personnel are competent at the basic-level tasks suited to their positions. As mentioned earlier, where they fail is in teaching and preparing their supervisors and managers to be effective leaders. Having reiterated this point, it's important to establish that any person who has authority and responsibility over other employees should also be technically competent in the tasks he is overseeing. While, with effective leadership skills, it is possible to overcome a lack of history, experience, or the ability to demonstrate technical competence in the basic skill, respect will be more difficult to attain from those subordinates.

So how does one gain the respect from his or her subordinates if one does not have the experience or competence of those he is overseeing? While I believe I was indeed technically competent in all the previous jobs I held, I always made it a point to attend and participate in training sessions with my subordinates. I wanted them to know that I hadn't forgotten what they were required to do, and that while I wasn't required to perform those tasks any longer, I still wanted to maintain a basic level of competence. I believe making this effort helped tremendously with establishing and maintaining a perception of competence with newer people who weren't part of the organization when I actually acted in their positions. It was important to me that they understood that I worked my way up through the ranks as opposed to simply being "born" as their boss.

As a senior chief, I would obviously respond to large incidents for command purposes or liaison duties with the elected and appointed officials. I would also respond to smaller emergencies and assist where necessary. This also helped maintain the perception that I still knew how to do the job and wasn't afraid to still engage. If there wasn't a task for me to perform at those emergencies, I would be quite happy to stand back and watch my people do the amazing work I could always count on them to do. This was probably my favorite part of being the fire chief. No matter how frustrated I may have been with the political aspect of my position, watching my people do their jobs filled me with pride and reminded me what my principle responsibility was: taking care of them.

Education

I strongly believe that for an individual to grow and continue to develop in life, education must be a constant. In addition, a leader must maintain an open mind and an actual willingness to learn. A leader understands that she doesn't know everything. Daniel J. Boorstin said, "Education is learning what you didn't even know you didn't know." Absent this attitude, becoming an effective leader will be nearly impossible.

Being professional comes with the expectation of being educated. Certainly, a leader will have to meet the minimum educational requirements for the position held within the organization. But does she stop there? Hopefully not. Be it the continuation of formal education, participation in outside career-track certifications, in-house skill-maintenance training, attendance at seminars and symposiums, keeping current with industry standards, or a combination thereof, the leader must continue the process of education.

With the advent of online formal education, obtaining a degree is more accessible than ever. Additionally, many trades and professions, such as the fire service, have state and federally sponsored or industry-accepted professional-development certification programs, some of which are mandated, many of which are not. Individual organizations that wisely see the advantages of investing in their people promote their own job-specific development programs.

A well-educated, professional leader benefits the organization greatly by possessing better instincts and critical-thinking skills, both of which result in better decision-making abilities. A professional leader takes every opportunity to improve as an individual and to serve as a positive role model. As the employees see their leaders demonstrate a philosophy of embracing continual education and professional development, they are generally inspired to follow suit and thus benefit the whole organization.

Self-Awareness

Are you truly aware of how effective you are as a supervisor, as a manager, and especially as a leader? How do you really know? Is it just a feeling? Is it based upon how well or poorly things are currently going at work? Or is it because you actually are self-aware enough to know the truth because you take the time to not only evaluate yourself but also to ask for the input of your subordinates, peers, and superiors? In my opinion, you can tell me anything you want as far as your effectiveness as a leader, but until I ask your employees, peers, and bosses, I'll take your words with a grain of salt. In other words, if you're not asking those who work with you on a regular basis for an honest evaluation of your effectiveness, you are not self-aware and are simply guessing as to your effectiveness.

Why do we, as professionals, need to be self-aware as to our effectiveness as leaders? The answer is, unless you know for a fact that you already are the perfect leader and no longer need to work to improve, how would you know what to work to improve on? The truth is, none of us are perfect as human beings, and by default, we are not perfect as supervisors, managers, and leaders. So if you believe in the need to practice the concept of continual improvement as a human being (hopefully, we all do), why wouldn't you believe in the concept of continual improvement as a leader? Logically, if we seek the input of those we live with for the purposes of improving as a human, why wouldn't we do the same for the purposes of improving as a supervisor, manager, and leader?

Wait a minute. If I ask my subordinates where I need to improve as a boss, doesn't that make me appear weak to them? Will they think that I'm really not as perfect as I profess to be? The answer is no. They already know you're not the perfect leader—get over yourself. You will gain much more respect by asking for their input, provided you are sincere about it and truly try to improve on your effectiveness. If you're not sincere, they'll see right through you.

It is important to remember that if your people don't trust you, you won't get honest feedback from them. If this is the case, you have more trouble than just being a poor supervisor, manager, or leader. You need to go back to the basics and work on becoming a trustworthy human being before trying to be an effective leader. For example; if they think you'll take their honest feedback and possibly use it against them down the road, they won't tell you the truth. If they think you're simply placating them and not serious about considering their feedback, you won't get the truth.

I am still a work-in-progress human being as well as a leader. Yes, even after many years as a human and as a leader, I still haven't reached perfection status. No, not even writing a book has made me perfect. I continually strive to improve in both of these areas of my life. I seek constructive criticism on a regular basis, both in my personal and professional lives, and try to apply it toward my efforts of continual improvement. I am aware that I need to work on becoming a more effective and patient listener. I am aware that I need to work on my ability to translate the thoughts in my head into clear, thorough, and complete messages before sending them out my mouth or putting them into written words. While this is certainly not a complete list (these are only two of the items I am currently working to improve upon), I am self-aware of what my current and ongoing shortcomings are as a human being and a leader. Are you?

Deportment

In this section of the book, I've discussed what I believe are the minimum requirements of a "professional" leader. I talked about the importance of proper appearance, effective communication skills, professional competence, education, and self-awareness. Next on the list is deportment, or how we carry ourselves as leaders.

This one is pretty simple to explain. If you have worked to master those previous four requirements of professionalism—appearance, communication skills, competence, and education—deportment will take care of itself. You will, by default, carry yourself with the self-confidence required of a leader, whether you're commanding an emergency, dealing with an administrative issue, making a formal presentation to a board of directors or a city council, or just walking into a room.

Let me clarify one thing. I said confidence; I did not say arrogance or cockiness. There is a huge difference. I used to tell my people that I wanted and needed them to carry themselves with the confidence they had earned through training and experience. Confidence that because of their training and experience they could handle any emergency they would encounter throughout their shift. Confidence that would be demonstrated through a strong command presence under extremely stressful situations. When people move through life behind a shield of arrogance or cockiness, I believe they are generally trying to hide from the fact that they are not confident in their own abilities. I believe these people are dangerous, especially in emergency or significant situations. These are the individuals who carry themselves confidently but without the competence to back it up. These are the individuals who will continue pushing a poor decision even though it is apparent to everyone else that the decision must be adjusted. These are also the individuals who are blinded by their cockiness and can't see that their emergency incident action plan isn't working and needs to be altered. That cockiness will get themselves or someone else seriously injured—or worse. I used to tell my people that the fence line between confidence and cockiness was narrow and sometimes tricky, but falling off that fence onto the cockiness side was extremely dangerous to them, their personnel, and the public they served.

Leaders Understand Politics

A quick internet search of definitions for "politics" reveals several applications of the word. Merriam-Webster alone has several applications. The broadest one states: "the total complex of relations between people living in society." What does this tell us? It tells us that if we are people, and we are living in society, we are dealing with politics. That kind of puts things in perspective. We don't have to be actual politicians; we're all dealing with politics, whether we realize it or not. Think about it: we're all strategizing or planning how to put ourselves in the right position to obtain what we need or want on a regular basis. We do this within our personal lives routinely. Then why do we tend to look at "playing politics" as a negative thing? Because like anything, lines can be crossed and people can be negatively affected—even in our personal lives. To this point, Merriam-Webster also states: "political activities characterized by artful and often dishonest practices." In my opinion, this applies to both our personal and work lives.

In this application, Merriam-Webster states: "political affairs or business: competition between competing interest groups or individuals for power and leadership." This is where politics directly applies to the subject matter of the book. The higher in an organization you advance as a supervisor, manager, and leader—in both the public and private sector—the greater the odds are that you will be subjected to the negative, or potentially negative, side of politics. For example, the different levels of politics I was exposed to from division chief to fire chief was unbelievable. To his credit, my predecessor was a master at handling politics. I see that now, but at the time I was observing him, I had no desire to attain that position. As a result, I didn't pay close enough attention or ask enough questions before he unexpectedly left the organization for professional opportunities elsewhere. I suddenly found myself exposed to an on-the-job crash course in heavy politics as an acting fire chief—during the Great Recession.

The public- and private-sector environments are different but still similar in many ways. In both environments, individuals are doing their best to position themselves for the next promotional spot or the most desirable position presently available to them. This means most are trying to look good in front of their bosses. Have you ever noticed that once a promotional opportunity is announced, several probable candidates start initiating special projects in hopes of gaining favor? On the other hand, negative rumors— usually without merit—may begin to flow in hopes of making someone look bad just prior to the promotion in order to make someone else look better. Two different scenarios: one acceptable, one not.

In both environments, senior positions are often suspended between the policy makers who hire and fire and the labor units who are obviously the ones that make the organization successful or profitable. The big bosses necessarily have to keep the policy makers happy with numbers, while making sure that labor feels supported, appreciated, and adequately compensated. This can be a huge challenge. For me as fire chief, it meant that I had to walk the line between not getting fired by the city manager or city council and not getting a vote of no confidence from the labor unit—all during the worst recession in memory, where city coffers were running low and the labor unit hadn't had a raise in years. In the end, I was successful in walking the line, but it wasn't easy. I endured sleepless nights, regular headaches, and two ulcers. Many times, traps were set for me, sometimes intentionally, sometimes by circumstance; sometimes political, sometimes personal— sometimes by people I expected and sometimes by those I didn't. By the way, much of this didn't become clear to me until after the dust settled, post-retirement.

As the big boss, you must be aware of the potential and real dangers of politics as you are promoted up the chain. You must also have a good idea of how to work your way through the mine field. Ideally, you want to understand the environment, operate within it, and keep yourself out of as many political traps as possible. Consider these ten points:

1.Don't accept an at-will or unrepresented senior leadership position without being of retirement age, or at least having negotiated a safety-net clause in your contract. At some point you'll most likely have to say "enough is enough" or "no, I'll quit before I do that." Additionally, you may in fact get fired, because, frankly, if you're doing your job, it's inevitable that at some point you're going to have to stand on your values, principles, and/or ethics and say, "no, I won't do that," which will frustrate the appointed or elected officials who hired you.

2. Understand your environment and where you are positioned within it. Who are your bosses? Are they elected or appointed officials who may set you up or allow you to take the fall for something they are responsible for—in order to keep their own position or to get reelected? Who are your peers and what are their desires and ambitions? Are there any potential hidden agendas? Who are your subordinates and what are their needs and desires? Do any of them have reason to set you up? At the same time, are you prepared

to   advocate for them and defend them if necessary? What are the potential political traps you may not see coming and find yourself caught in?

3. Reference organizational guiding documents on a regular basis, and always do so when faced with a significant decision. The answers to the vast majority of your questions or dilemmas are there as well as the justifications to defend those decisions.

4. Have a decision-making matrix that includes an ethical filter and be willing to use it on a regular basis. Also understand that you will never gain 100 percent approval for any significant decision you make, ever.

5. Blindly trust no one. Everyone has some semblance of a political agenda, and it may be hidden from you. In other words, you may be surprised at what some people will do to get ahead.

6. Be comfortable listening to and considering your intuition, that little voice. Remember, it's based on your life experiences, your lifelong education, and your training. It's right more often than not.

7. With all else being equal, err on the side of your people. They're the ones who are making you look good and your organization successful. If you truly are an effective leader, they're also the ones who will have your back.

8. Understand that your reputation and level of organizational respect begins the day you walk into your agency or company. Don't give anyone future ammunition to use against you. When you are promoted, every little bit of negativity associated with your career will be brought up and considered for use against you in the political arena.

9. Pay attention to the next position in your career ladder. Learn all you can about it, especially any political ramifications. It will pay big dividends for you when you reach that level. Additionally, don't be afraid to say, "that position is not for me, at least until I'm at my retirement age."

10. Stay focused on your realm of responsibility. You're now paid to think about the big picture or the strategy of the organization. You're not paid to think at the tactical or task level. Your job is to focus on the vision and how to get there, which means you have to consider the politics involved in everything you do.

Leaders Pursue the Organizational Vision with a Plan and an Inspired Team

If an organization is to improve, two things must happen: First, a current organizational vision and associated goals to meet that vision must be created to establish a direction or destination for the leaders to take the company. Second, the leaders must transition their "groups" of individuals into "teams" of individuals who are inspired to complete those goals and ultimately achieve the vision.

Any organization that desires to improve itself has a list of goals that need to be accomplished that will lead to their vision being achieved. Public-sector agencies or private-sector businesses should have a vision for the future. (Whether they choose to actually follow that plan and pursue and attain the vision is a different thing altogether.) A private-sector company must improve, or they will fail. As a result, the vast majority have a vision and aggressively work toward it, if for no other reason than survival. Unfortunately, too many public-sector agencies—which don't depend on profit to survive—become content with the status quo. As such, they simply meet the daily mission without chasing a current vision for improvement. This is a sad and disappointing thing to me, since these public agencies are funded by taxpayer dollars. They seem to forget that we are all taxpayers and deserve better than the status quo.

Leaders must fully understand and buy in to their organization's strategic or business plan. These plans not only state the foundational mission and core values of the organization but clearly state the current vision and the goals that need to be completed to achieve it. If a leader's purpose is to inspire his people to work toward and achieve the vision, how could he fulfill that purpose without a current plan? The leader must also refer to the vision and the plan on a regular basis with his or her people to ensure that it remains in the forefront. I should also add that the strategic or business plan must be current. Many public-sector agencies have strategic or business plans that, after significant effort in developing them, simply sit on a shelf and become obsolete.

In the fire service, the concept of a "leader's intent" is a critical aspect of bringing an emergency incident to a safe conclusion. It is imperative that the officer in charge quickly develops a strategic incident action plan for the emergency. He or she then makes the appropriate tactical assignments to support the strategy of the plan. If the incident commander chooses to make these tactical assignments without advising the subordinate officers of the primary elements of the plan (the leader's intent), tactical objectives are likely not to be carried out in a manner that supports the plan. This is how unnecessary property damage occurs. This is also how firefighters are injured or killed. However, if the incident commander does share his or her incident action plan with the subordinate officers, the incident will more than likely be mitigated safely and more efficiently. It is only logical that the subordinate officers will make better decisions if they understand what the overall plan is for the incident.

The same principle applies during nonemergency or routine business operations. The leaders must regularly share their plans with everyone in the organization or within their area of responsibility. Remember, the idea is to give them the plan, support them, and let them use their own creativity and ingenuity to get the job done. In doing so, they move the organization forward.

A strategic or business plan gives an organization a sense of purpose and direction and poses crucial questions. "Why are we here? What is our purpose? What values do we hold dear? What are the current issues and how do we overcome them? Where are we going, and what will we look like when we get there?" It is the critical document that leaders at all levels of the organization focus and rely on so they can gauge where they place their time and efforts as they relate to their employees.

In the private sector, companies wouldn't dream of existing without a current strategic or business plan to help guide them to success and profitability. Why then do some public agencies think they can be successful or improve without a plan? The costs are high when we do this. Low morale among the employees and low customer or citizen satisfaction are usually the results. They become status quo, or worse yet, mediocre public agencies.

A strategic or business plan is not a pretty book that sits on a shelf. It is not a document that is looked at every five years in order to be updated. It is not, nor should it ever be, a complicated document that no one refers to, no one understands, and whose contents no one can remember.

A strategic or business plan should not be a secret document for upper management personnel only. It is the guiding document that everyone in the organization has (hopefully) contributed to. It is a working document to which everyone in the organization has access.

A strategic or business plan is a living, breathing, dynamic, guiding document that is referred to by an organization on a daily basis for direction and decision making. It should be continually updated as progress is made or as adjustments become necessary.

It tells us what we are expected to do each day. It tells us what priority organizational issues should be worked on today in order to achieve the vision of tomorrow.

Some organizations may find it necessary to build elaborate strategic or business plans. That is also fine but totally unnecessary. A good working strategic or business plan can be very simple and basic. The critical element is that the plan is regularly referred to and adhered to. Remember, this is a working document, not a showpiece.

Some organizations prefer to put a multiyear plan together and only update at the end of the multiyear period. Having a multiyear plan is a good idea; however, it should be continually reviewed and updated as progress is made. The document should always be up to date and current.

However, in the end, when the so-called leaders of the organization are resistant to the benefits of such a plan, that organization's future is imperiled. When you work for or with people who are unwilling to commit to the value of a strategic or business plan, to follow and refer to it on a regular basis and keep it current, there is really no reason to put the effort into the process. If they are willing to be content with the status quo and uninterested in moving the organization forward, the process will be a waste of everyone's time and energy.

The basic building block of every organization is the individual. They look at problems and solutions differently. Individuals bring a diversity of life experiences, talents, and ideas to an organization. They consist of both genders and come from different cultural and socioeconomic environments. Their ages differ and therefore bring a variety of generational values. Their diversity is the strength of the organization.

How successful do you think an organization of all like-minded individuals would be? Not very, in my opinion. Any organization that wants to be successful should embrace diversity in its hiring process for the reasons mentioned above. Yes, in the perfect world the demographic diversity of a community should be reflected in its workforce. However, the benefit is not in simply focusing on demographics. The advantage is the by-product of embracing demographic diversity, which are the functional benefits that result from it. Benefits such as increased ingenuity, creativeness, and problem-solving abilities are the true advantages to a successful company.

When an organization recognizes the advantages of placing these diverse individuals into groups under a common mission, and subsequently under effective supervisors and managers, the diversity of those individuals combines to strengthen that organization and allow it to effectively meet the mission on a daily basis. Meeting the mission of any organization is extremely important, and is in fact the minimum requirement for the continued existence of that organization and its ability to maintain the status quo. While maintaining the status quo is necessary, most organizations will not be satisfied with this. This is where the leader is truly needed and appreciated.

A leader transforms a group of individuals into a team by developing synergy between one another that results from each individual's self-motivation. This synergy is inspired by the leader, and it can be leveraged to encourage individuals to work together, accomplish goals, and pursue the organizational vision to fruition—as a team. I said leaders must inspire their people, not motivate them. I believe that only the individual can truly motivate himself to accomplish something. The best a leader can do is inspire the individual to self-motivate. A group of self-motivated individuals working together—following the strategic business plan—to chase a vision with their inspirational leaders is no longer just a group, they are a functionally diverse, problem-solving, vision-attaining, synergetic team.

What is synergy? Synergy is that magic element that develops between energized individuals that makes them stronger and more effective as a team than they are as single employees. How do we develop synergy? We follow the suggestions in this book! It really is that simple, and it really is that difficult at the same time. It's simple because the answers are here, in one place. I'm not saying that I have all the answers. I'm saying that if you develop yourself as a supervisor, manager, and especially a leader by using the concepts in this book, you will have the tools and ability to convert your group of employees into a team of talented, creative, innovative, inspired individuals who want the team and the organization to succeed. It's also difficult because your development as a leader, as well as the group's transition to a team, will take time and dedication. It won't happen overnight, and it won't happen by itself. Unfortunately, as I've stated previously, most organizations—unless you are the actual boss—won't help you through this process. However, in the end, there is no other way to develop an effective team but through time, hard work, and the ongoing dedication of the leader.

Leading through the "Fog of War"

Up to this point in the chapter, I've been focusing on what a supervisor or manager can learn to become a leader, someone with the intention of inspiring his or her team to accomplish the goals necessary to attain the organizational vision. This is not to be taken lightly. Leading a team to attain a vision is huge. So many organizations never accomplish this, especially in the public sector. However, the assumption here is that this "leading" is done under normal, everyday conditions. What about when conditions exist that are not normal? What about critical or emergency conditions? What is required of the leader during the fog of war?

What is the fog of war? For me, it is the confusing, stressful times of crisis—difficult economic or budgetary periods, natural or manmade disasters, and, of course, being in a literal battle. Obviously these are very general examples. You may experience more specific examples in your area of responsibility within your organization. Regardless, as long as you are experiencing confusing, stressful times, you're in the fog of war.

Leading during the fog of war is the ultimate test of a leader. Former University of Texas Head Football Coach Mack Brown said, "Leadership is poise under pressure." The good news is, if you possess and practice the tools of a leader, such as those I've discussed in this book, you will have the ability to lead your people through the fog of war. The key here is to be able to step back and recognize that you truly are in confusing and stressful times. Once this is recognized, you need to understand your position and responsibility within the organization, see the big picture, calmly and confidently identify the issues, prioritize them, develop a plan with your team to overcome the situation, share the plan with your team (leader's intent), and then lead them through it. Everyone around you will be caught up in the situation and reacting to the circumstances, but nothing will get done without a leader and a plan. That, my friend, is where you come in. In Simon Sinek's book, *Leaders Eat Last*, retired US Marine Lieutenant General George J. Flynn says it best: "I know of no case study in history that describes an organization that has been managed out of a crisis. Every single one of them was led."

On January 1, 2010, shortly before midnight, I received the notification from dispatch that every public-safety chief dreads. While this wasn't my first personnel-injury notification (unfortunately, an all-too-common occurrence in the public-safety world), this one was different. The notification said, "May-day called; two firefighters through the roof and trapped." Indeed, this is what had occurred. Two members of one of our ladder truck companies were attempting to vertically ventilate (open the roof to release the heat and smoke in an effort to make conditions easier on the engine companies attacking the fire from below) over a garage fire, when the roof structure collapsed underneath them, and they dropped into the inferno below. They were both entangled in the debris. One of them was able to self-extricate, but the other was not. While he was only trapped approximately ninety seconds before being rescued, he sustained third-degree burns over the majority of his body and was not expected to survive.

While responding to the incident, the realization that I was ultimately responsible for everything that happened in my fire department set in. The fact that I had only been acting fire chief for a couple of months didn't matter. I was in the seat now and, by default, responsible. The feeling was so overwhelming that I had to pull to the side of the road and regain my composure. Several questions raced through my head: How did this happen? What did I miss? What did I fail to do? Where did I go wrong? Over the years in the department, I had served in many different roles, most with influence on or responsibilities to our policies and procedures. I was in charge of the training division, a shift battalion chief, the emergency operations division chief, and now the acting fire chief. My fingerprints were all over our fire ground operations. While I did my best to keep my people as safe as possible in a perpetually dangerous occupation, the ultimate effectiveness of my work was now staring me in the face. In an instant, my responsibilities had become vividly real. I loved my people and wanted nothing more than to keep them safe.

I arrived at the fire just as my two firefighters were being loaded into the ambulances. I clearly remember the vacant, stunned, concerned, and even scared look of the other crews. I remember walking up to the incident commander (who, by the way, did an excellent job handling the emergency). I looked at his face, and I realized that neither one of us could speak at that moment. We just hugged. I also remember that later, as the sun was coming up, I walked over to the burned protective gear that was removed from the two firefighters and stared. The realization that my people were actually wearing that gear, carrying out the mission of my fire department, became overwhelming, and I had to turn to vomit. The burden of leadership was real.

I don't want to take this story any further before I tell you that both firefighters survived. The most seriously burned firefighter not only survived, but after months of countless surgeries and painful procedures, returned to full duty. I stand in awe of this remarkable human being with an unbelievable will to survive. One of the greatest days of my life was being privileged enough to watch him hang his gear back on the same ladder truck company that he was assigned to the night of that horrific incident. He later retired, under his own terms and conditions.

The next morning, shortly after notifying Cal-OSHA of the incident, the acting deputy city manager and I had a short conversation about where we would go after this in regard to an investigation. Would we handle it internally? Should we bring in outside experts? We quickly realized that, as painful and exhaustive as this would be, we needed to open this investigation up to the outside. We brought in fire service experts from throughout central and northern California to investigate. We also assigned a member of the firefighters' labor unit to the team to ensure transparency in the process for our local members. We wanted not only to find out what went wrong but also, more importantly, to know how we could prevent this from reoccurring—not just in my fire department but in all fire departments in the country. I quickly realized that this experience was already testing—and would continue to test—my ability to lead this organization through the fog of war.

For six months, we supported two very thorough and invasive external investigations into this incident: one from the Cal-OSHA Enforcement Branch, and the other from the Multi-Agency Accident Investigation Team. In June 2010, we were notified by Cal-OSHA that there were no applicable state worker safety laws violated and that there would be no fines issued. I give full credit for this to our organization's willingness several years earlier to invite the Cal-OSHA Consultation Branch into our department to evaluate our policies, procedures, and practices to ensure we were compliant with state law.

We were also notified by the Multi-Agency Accident Investigation Team that they had numerous recommendations related to industry best practices for us to implement as a result of their investigation. At that point, I took a deep breath and told myself, "Here's where the rubber meets the road." Was I ready to share our shortcomings, mistakes, errors, oversights, overconfidence, and lapses in judgement as a department—most of which had my fingerprints all over them—with the world? Could I maintain the priority of this task against other priorities that we were facing, such as the recession and a rapidly shrinking budget with looming layoffs? Could I, as I had preached for years, admit our mistakes, learn from them, and not repeat them? Did I have the ability to convince my people that we needed to reevaluate everything we did operationally and then lead them through the process of change? Did I have the ability to not only endure the embarrassment of taking full responsibility as the current fire chief but also convince the elected officials and taxpayers that I could be trusted to complete this massive undertaking? Bottom line, could I lead through the fog of war? The answer to these questions was clear: I had to.

I had to for all my firefighters. I had to for all firefighters throughout the country and the world. I had to for my citizens who pay our salaries, and I most certainly had to do it for my two recovering firefighters who were injured that night operating under my policies and procedures as the acting fire chief.

We quickly went before the local media to present the report, answer questions, admit our mistakes, and most importantly, commit to learning from those mistakes and fully implementing the resulting recommendations. We then went to work as an inspired team with a clear vision of taking this organization to the next level of operational efficiency and safety.

Two years later, and just months before I retired, I was able to go before my organization—with my two injured firefighters sitting in the audience—now as their regular fire chief, and list how each of those recommendations in the report had been fully researched, vetted, and implemented within our fire department guiding documents.

Knowing that my entire tenure as fire chief was in a "fog of war," including shrinking revenues and collapsing budgets, a perpetual fight to prevent layoffs, working to merge three fire departments into one, and—worst of all—almost losing two of my firefighters, I cherish the memory of sitting before the most important element of my organization—my people—and letting them know that their safety and ability to go home to their families the next morning always was and continued to be my top priority.

It is important to remember that during their tenure, very few bosses are allowed the privilege of leading their people without having to do so in some semblance of the fog of war. Recognition of and adherence to the basic concepts of being a supervisor, manager, and, most importantly, a leader, such as are listed in this book and in many other places, will certainly help in the process, just as they did me during the Great Recession and the near loss of my two firefighters.

Workbook for Leaders

Leadership Capabilities

An individual must have the desire—not just the capability—to become a leader.

Do you want to be a leader?

_____

_____

How can I improve?

_____

_____

_____

_____

_____

_____

_____

_____

_____

_____

_____

_____

_____

_____

_____

_____

As a leader, do you have the ability to inspire your people to move above and beyond the status quo and attain the vision for the future?

_____

_____

How can I improve?

_____

_____

_____

_____

_____

_____

_____

_____

_____

_____

_____

_____

_____

_____

_____

_____

_____

_____

_____

Act Like a Leader

The traits of a leader include integrity, courage, decisiveness, dependability, responsibility, initiative, tact, fairness, enthusiasm, loyalty, and consistency.

Do you demonstrate these?

_____

_____

Better yet, do your people believe you demonstrate these qualities?

_____

_____

Additionally, are you willing to work on those traits that you may be weak in?

_____

_____

How can I improve?

_____

_____

_____

_____

_____

_____

_____

Leaders Appreciate Their People

Leaders appreciate their people and express it to them on a regular basis.

Do you?

_____

_____

How can I improve?

_____

_____

_____

_____

_____

_____

_____

_____

_____

_____

_____

_____

_____

_____

_____

_____

Leaders Appreciate Their Organization's History

Leaders appreciate their organization's history and pass it on to their people.

Do you?

_____

_____

How can I improve?

_____

_____

_____

_____

_____

_____

_____

_____

_____

_____

_____

_____

_____

_____

_____

_____

_____

The Four Cs of Leadership

Leaders understand the four Cs of leadership: Commitment, Communication, Collaboration, and Compromise.

Are you committed to the organization and its people?

_____

_____

Do you communicate in all directions?

_____

_____

Do you utilize the ingenuity and creativity of your people by collaborating with them?

_____

_____

Are you willing to compromise on issues for the good of the organization?

_____

_____

_____

_____

_____

_____

_____

How can I improve?

_____

_____

_____

_____

_____

_____

_____

_____

_____

_____

_____

_____

_____

_____

_____

_____

_____

_____

_____

_____

_____

_____

Leaders Train their People

Leaders train their people and give them the tools they need to meet their mission.

Do you understand that by developing your people, you improve their effectiveness, which in-turn increases the organization's level of success?

_____

_____

Additionally, do you continually develop yourself?

_____

_____

How can I improve?

_____

_____

_____

_____

_____

_____

_____

_____

_____

_____

_____

A Leader's Decision-Making Process

Leaders develop and utilize effective decision-making processes for both emergency and nonemergency situations. Leaders trust themselves when making significant decisions.

Do you?

_____

_____

How can I improve?

_____

_____

_____

_____

_____

_____

_____

_____

_____

_____

_____

_____

_____

Leaders Understand the Power of Yes and No

Leaders understand the power of saying yes and that of saying no. They understand the importance of utilizing both words, the appropriateness of both words, and the impact they have on their people and the organization.

Do you?

_____

_____

How can I improve?

_____

_____

_____

_____

_____

_____

_____

_____

_____

_____

_____

_____

_____

_____

_____

Leaders Understand that They Can't Do It All

Leaders know they can't do it all, and, as a result, they delegate effectively. They are careful not to abuse this right and to maintain an awareness of their people's workload. And they clearly set the parameters of the delegated assignment.

Do you?

_____

_____

How can I improve?

_____

_____

_____

_____

_____

_____

_____

_____

_____

_____

_____

_____

_____

_____

Leaders Act as Professionals

Leaders are professionals in appearance, communication, competence, education, self-awareness, and deportment.

Are you?

_____

_____

Do you dress appropriately for your position?

_____

_____

Do you continually work on your communication abilities, including oral, written, and listening?

_____

_____

Do you demonstrate competence in your area of responsibility?

_____

_____

Do you continually strive to increase your education?

_____

_____

_____

Are you truly self-aware as to your effectiveness as a leader?

_____

_____

Do you demonstrate a leader's confidence, while being very careful not to become arrogant?

_____

_____

How can I improve?

_____

_____

_____

_____

_____

_____

_____

_____

_____

_____

_____

_____

_____

_____

_____

Leaders Understand Politics

Leaders understand that there are politics at play in most organizations, and the higher one moves upward, the more one will be exposed to politics.

Do you?

_____

_____

How can I improve?

_____

_____

_____

_____

_____

_____

_____

_____

_____

_____

_____

_____

_____

_____

Leaders understand that because politics do exist in the workplace, one must have an ethical decision-making filter that must be used on a regular basis.

Do you?

_____

_____

How can I improve?

_____

_____

_____

_____

_____

_____

_____

_____

_____

_____

_____

_____

_____

Leaders understand that one must be aware, equipped, and prepared to accept a position exposed to a heavy level of politics.

Do you?

_____

_____

How can I improve?

_____

_____

_____

_____

_____

_____

_____

_____

_____

_____

_____

_____

_____

_____

_____

_____

_____

_____

Leaders understand that, at some point while holding a position exposed to a heavy level of politics, one may have to say, "no, I will not go there," and be prepared to leave the position.

Do you?

_____

_____

How can I improve?

_____

_____

_____

_____

_____

_____

_____

_____

_____

_____

_____

_____

_____

_____

_____

_____

Leaders Pursue the Organizational Vision with a Plan and an Inspired Team

Leaders recognize the value of a diverse group of individuals and the advantages they bring to the organization.

Do you?

_____

_____

How can I improve?

_____

_____

_____

_____

_____

_____

_____

_____

_____

_____

_____

_____

_____

_____

_____

Leaders ensure that the vision and the plan are always current. They refer to the vision and the plan on a regular basis and communicate the "leader's intent" to their people.

Do you?

_____

_____

How can I improve?

_____

_____

_____

_____

_____

_____

_____

_____

_____

_____

_____

_____

_____

_____

_____

_____

_____

Leaders inspire their people and create a synergy between them that converts a group of individuals into an innovative, creative, and driven team pursing the organizational vision.

Do you?

_____

_____

How can I improve?

_____

_____

_____

_____

_____

_____

_____

_____

_____

_____

_____

_____

_____

_____

_____

_____

_____

Leading through the "Fog of War"

Leaders understand that the ultimate test of their abilities comes during confusing and stressful periods.

Do you have the knowledge, skills, and abilities to step back and recognize confusing and stressful times, understand your position and responsibility within your organization, calmly and confidently gather the facts and see the big picture, develop a plan to overcome the situation, share the plan with your team (leader's intent), and lead them through it?

_____

_____

Do you?

_____

_____

How can I improve?

_____

_____

_____

_____

_____

_____

_____

_____

Conclusion

Congratulations on making it to this portion of the book!

You've taken an important first step in developing into an effective supervisor, manager, and, most importantly, leader. Now what? Well, now that you have the knowledge, the next step is to begin to honestly evaluate yourself. I strongly suggest that you go back and read the book again. This time, go to the workbook area immediately following each chapter and begin evaluating how well you believe you currently exemplify these concepts. Once you began to honestly recognize your shortfalls, you should be able to write down how you can improve. You can then regularly refer to that section of the book to gauge your progress as you begin applying what you've learned. Make it a practice to periodically review the book and adjust your notes as you continue to develop.

Just reading the book once will not do the trick. This book is simply a foundation for you to build upon. You must understand that this will not be an overnight process. In fact, this will be a perpetual-development process that will continue as long as you are driven to improve.

My motivation behind writing this book was to inspire you—the current or future supervisor, manager, and leader in your organization—to feel the passion to not only improve yourself but to also develop those supervisors, managers, and leaders who are coming up behind you. If, along the way, you happen to inspire your bosses to improve, great. They aren't my focus; you are. Any hope for a better future in your organization is in your hands and in those who will follow you. Good luck!

Oh, and one more thing: please do your best to maintain a positive work-life balance. This book will indeed help you become more productive and will allow you to accomplish much more than you believed you could as a boss. However, the book is not intended to suggest that you transform into a workaholic.

Life is short. Don't shorten it even more by working to the point that you don't enjoy life or you create health problems for yourself. Even if you remain healthy, and I hope you do, take adequate time off for rest and relaxation. Do things you enjoy with friends and family. Strive to live a full and satisfying life and fill it with great memories.

Yes, we all have to work, and we all want to be successful, but please remember, at the end of your life, before you take your last breath, your most cherished memories shouldn't be about work.